Experiences for
Teaching
Children Mathematics

Experiences for Teaching Children Mathematics

LEONARD M. KENNEDY

CALIFORNIA STATE UNIVERSITY, SACRAMENTO

WADSWORTH PUBLISHING COMPANY, INC.

BELMONT, CALIFORNIA

Editors: Sandra Craig / Sandra Mangurian
Designer, calligrapher, and text illustrator: Dave Comstock
Cover Designer: Courtney Boie

ISBN: 0-534-00217-X
L.C. Catalog Card Number: 72-87808
Printed in the United States of America
   2 3 4 5 6 7 8 9 10 —— 77 76 75 74 73

To keep the price of this book as low as possible, we have used an
economical means of typesetting. We welcome your comments.

Preface

SINCE 1960 dramatic changes occurred in both the content and the
methods of teaching mathematics in the elementary school. New topics
have been added and old ones have shifted, usually from higher to lower
levels in school. Materials and instructional procedures have also
changed.

The changes in content, materials, and procedures have altered the
role of the teacher. Where formerly he stood before his class each day
to instruct the children on processes, today the teacher finds that he
uses this mode of teaching much less frequently. Instead, his mode of
teaching shifts from day to day. One time he works with the whole class
to help them understand a concept. Another time he works with children
in small groups or singly as they pursue topics in which they are interested. More and more he works in a laboratory setting. Here he responds
to children's needs by furnishing equipment and supplies, by organizing
the room for efficient learning, by suggesting topics and procedures for
investigations, by questioning and responding to questions, and by guiding children's learning experiences in many other ways.

Experiences for Teaching Children Mathematics offers a variety
of activities to help you prepare to teach mathematics. As you do these
activities, you will find that you fill the role of both learner and
teacher. You will be a learner as you complete sequences of program-
type activities, watch as a fellow student demonstrates to you how he
uses a teaching aid, or perform activities at a learning center. You
will be a teacher as you demonstrate how you use a teaching aid, prepare
problem cards, or plan a learning center.

Chapter 1 contains readings that give you an overview of mathematics
in schools today. The activities in Chapter 2 acquaint you with performance
objectives for mathematics. Chapters 3 through 7 contain some elementary school mathematics topics and procedures for teaching them. Chapter
3 describes teacher-directed activities for helping children understand
whole numbers. In Chapter 4 you will learn one way to set up learning
centers that deal with fractional numbers. Activities in Chapter 5 center on problem cards and models for geometry. Chapter 6 treats multimedia devices and measurement, and finally, Chapter 7 includes games and
experiments for teaching about probability, statistics, and logic.

The roles you play as you complete the activities in this book are
busy ones, and they may not always be easy ones. The experiences you
have as you play these roles will prepare you for the more difficult role
you are yet to play--that of being a teacher of mathematics. Good luck.

Contents

Experiences for
Teaching
Children Mathematics

1

Mathematics Today

A DECADE ago magazines bearing articles titled "Is Your Child Learning
the 'New' Mathematics?" and "We Are Experiencing a New Revolution—The
Revolution in Mathematics" appeared on newsstands. These articles usually
dealt with new content—sets and set notation, geometry, logic—and new
ways of looking at old content—Cartesian products in multiplication and a
different procedure for doing long division. They exerted considerable
influence on the changing scene in elementary school mathematics. For one
thing, they hastened the rate of change. Parents who were dissatisfied
with their children's progress saw opportunities for improvement, and many
became impatient for change. Even though they did not always understand
all of what they read, they urged their schools to adopt new programs.
Others, of course, resisted change; they were satisfied with the "old"
mathematics.

Teachers and administrators had the same feelings. Some quickly became
familiar with the recommendations of mathematicians, who initially were in
the majority of those urging change, and of mathematics educators, and programs began to change in many schools. There were also teachers and administrators who resisted change.

In the second decade since modern mathematics programs appeared, most
parents, teachers, and administrators recognize that contemporary programs
are superior to those of the past. Do you think we will ever go back to
the "old" mathematics? is a question seldom asked any more. The answer
has been and will continue to be no. Neither will we be content with pro-

grams that remain static, as has been true in the past, no matter how "modern" they are. Although it is unlikely that we will ever completely understand the learning process so that we can establish once and for all a program of instruction suitable for all children, we recognize that we can apply the best knowledge presently available to give them the best learning experiences possible. At the same time we continue to search for better understanding of how learning takes place, so that we can keep improving our programs.

The articles that follow give insights into the nature of contemporary programs, the learning theories upon which they are based, and the setting in which they take place. In the first article, Harold Lerch identifies seven ways in which contemporary programs differ from those of the past. Although his discussion is brief, you will gain a better understanding of mathematics in today's elementary schools and the reasons for changes that have occurred.

What is a Contemporary Elementary Mathematics Program? HAROLD H. LERCH

INQUIRE at almost any elementary school about the math program and you will most likely be told that a modern elementary mathematics program is being taught in that school system. The response will usually be supported by such statements as these:

"The system is using a recently published textbook series."

"Units of work dealing with sets, geometry, systems of numeration with bases other than ten, properties of number, and so forth are being taught at various instructional levels."

"Teachers have recently attended an inservice workshop in modern mathematics."

"The system has invested a substantial amount of money in instructional materials and aids."

But after analyzing the program on the basis of desirable characteristics of contemporary mathematics programs, you may well reach the disturbing conclusion that the program is contemporary only in the sense that it currently exists. Physical attributes—which might include a new textbook series, units of work dealing with content new to the elementary curriculum, inservice workshops for teachers, and instructional materials and aids—contribute to the *possibility* of a contemporary mathematics program. They do not, however, assure that there is a contemporary program.

What, then, is a contemporary mathematics program? It is impossible to offer a definition in a few sentences or in a few paragraphs. Each of the articles in this volume defines and describes important aspects of the program and states or implies their interrelationships. One might respond to the question, however, by discussing two related questions: How should current programs differ from programs of the past? What type of involvement—on the part of pupils, teachers, and administrators—is required if the mathematics program is to serve its objectives effectively?

Differences and Similarities

Contemporary mathematics programs and the arithmetic programs of yesterday are more different than they are similar. Similarities exist only in some of the objectives and in the arithmetic content. Contemporary programs differ from programs of the past in these ways:

Psychological foundations. Changing views of how children learn have influenced the selection, organization, and sequence of content, as well as the instructional procedures used.

Program objectives. Contemporary programs retain the objectives of earlier arithmetic programs. These are objectives concerned with developing understanding of our system of numeration, concepts of quantity and quantitative relationships, skill in computation, and ability to think in quantitative situations and to solve the problems of present and future everyday living. In addition, however, modern programs strive to help each child understand the structure of mathematics, its laws and principles, its sequences and order, and the way in which mathematics as a system expands to meet new needs. They also try to develop independent thinking processes and to help each child prepare for the next steps in mathematical learning that are appropriate for him in terms of his potential and his future educational requirements.

Scope of content. The scope of the content of elementary mathematics programs has been expanded to include mathematics that has not previously been taught at the elementary level. Thus, pupils are now expected to gain a knowledge of the real number system and the main ideas of geometry in the elementary grades. This new content is included in contemporary programs not as

fragmented parts or merely because children *can* learn it. Rather, it is included to help children begin to develop an understanding of the structure of mathematics and to give them a basis for understanding and utilizing the relationships of the integrated field. Emphasis is on major mathematical ideas rather than on isolated facts, rules, and manipulations.

Organization of content. In modern programs, major concepts are introduced at earlier levels and spirally developed at later stages. As the topic arises with increasing complexity at later levels, provision is made for each child to expand his understanding, knowledge, and application of the concept. Emphasis is upon the search for patterns and upon understanding relationships between concepts. Content is organized around topics, concepts, and relationships of importance or enduring value, including number and numeration, properties of number, operations, geometry, and measurement.

Instructional procedures. There is current consensus that the inductive approach, or the discovery method, is more conducive to developmental learning and to retention than is an instructional process based on presentation of rules and facts by the teacher. In programs of the past, the teacher's role was to explain and demonstrate; the pupil's role was to memorize facts, rules, and manipulations. Pupils were passive recipients of information, while teachers emphasized "telling." All this has changed in good contemporary programs to a teaching-learning process in which pupils are guided by teachers to discover for themselves the basic structural elements, concepts, and interrelationships of mathematics. As a result, the role of the teacher has now become one of structuring learning situations, guiding, questioning, diagnosing, and encouraging active pupil participation in the learning process. The role of the pupil now stresses observing, recording and collecting evidence, checking hunches, organizing relevant data, and formulating conclusions. A modern instructional approach includes, among other things, developing and using the language of mathematics; forming and exploring concepts through the use of concrete and illustrative materials; using different approaches when topics are reintroduced at successive levels of difficulty; adjusting instruction to the learning styles, pace, and achievement of individual pupils; and accepting from pupils various possible correct solutions to quantitative problems.

Applications. In the past, arithmetic programs sought to develop in pupils the skills and knowledge that would enable them to solve everyday problems and to handle the quantitative problems they encountered in their other academic endeavors. While these applications are still considered to be valid for a contemporary program, the skill and knowledge requirements for making such applications have changed. New and developing programs in the sciences and social studies, for example, often demand a kind of mathematics quite different from the mathematics pupils were taught in the old arithmetic. Contemporary programs must take these new requirements into account if they are to be applicable to pupils' needs. In a contemporary program, applications should pertain to present and future everyday life situations, to other academic disciplines, and to the utilization of mathematical concepts within the field of mathematics itself.

Evaluation. The evaluation of modern elementary mathematics programs cannot be based upon pupils' ability to recall facts and rules and to perform operations mechanically. Previously described changes in the program objectives and teaching-learning processes require modifications in the nature of evaluation. Evaluation procedures must be directed toward ascertaining pupils' understanding of facts, generalizations, and operations; their ability to apply mathematical skills and concepts in situations removed from the mathematics class. In regard to the total program, consideration must be given to how well it succeeds in achieving the broad objectives established for pupils and to how it compares with alternative types of programs in meeting these objectives.

Need for Involvement

The possibilities of what can be accomplished in a contemporary elementary mathematics program are directly related to the nature and extent of the involvement of pupils, teachers, and administrators. Modern elementary mathematics programs are *active* programs. Activity is not limited to pupil participation in learning experiences of an inductive or discovery nature and to the use of more and more instructional aids and materials. It extends to the involvement of administrators and teachers in efforts to expand their knowledge of content, instructional procedures, and organizational techniques and to their continuous efforts to improve the program.

. . . .

Teacher involvement is critical. The elementary mathematics program is in the hands of classroom teachers; if it falls, it will be at their feet. Moreover, it is not inappropriate to consider what a mathematics program can do for teachers to help them become better teachers. The role of the teacher in a modern program is not a passive one of standing back and letting children discover. The teacher can learn more about the unique characteristics of his pupils and be better prepared to adjust instruction to those differences through active participation in selecting appropriate learning experiences, structuring and guiding, and working with individuals. Many teachers may learn more mathematics through teaching in a modern program or participating in in-service programs than they thought they were capable of learning—or interested in learning. Their attitudes toward mathematics may change in a favorable direction. Professional growth in knowledge of the mathematics content of the total program and of appropriate instructional procedures and materials can result from active involvement in a modern program.

Although many recent publications concentrate on what contemporary mathematics programs can do for talented children, modern programs should be directed toward *all* pupils. Unless the program helps all children to learn mathematics better and more efficiently than they would in a traditional approach, it can hardly be called modern. One of the most self-degrading characteristics we can give to the adult of the future is to make him dependent upon others for interpreting quantitative data necessary to his occupational endeavors and to the decisions he must make as an active citizen in a technological society. Modern programs can and should provide opportunities for all pupils to achieve appropriate individual educational and vocational objectives. The content being stud-

ied and the goals for pupils may differ, but the extent of their active participation in the learning experiences of the program should be similar. In a good contemporary program, all pupils will be exploring, observing, testing hypotheses, and generalizing in their development of the language, concepts, structures, and techniques of mathematics.

An integral part of the contemporary elementary mathematics program is planned change. It is reasonable to believe that further modification will occur in the content and instructional procedures of existing and future programs. The sources of possible change are as numerous as the individuals—pupils, teachers, administrators, consultants, researchers, theorists—who are actively involved. Beware of the contemporary program as it becomes settled or stationary. The stationary program of today becomes the inadequate traditional program of tomorrow.

The view of contemporary programs in Lerch's article is a broad one. In the article that follows, Lloyd Scott considers change from a narrower point of view as he discusses theories of learning. First he gives a brief glimpse of how learning has been viewed in the past. He points out that beginning in about 1935 the "meaning theory" began to replace former theories. This theory remains but is influenced by three persons—Jean Piaget, Jerome Bruner, and Z. P. Dienes. Finally Scott gives ten themes related to various views of learning. All educators do not agree wholly with all the themes—and you may be among those who disagree—but you should be aware of them so that you can understand contemporary programs.

The Changing View of Learning   LLOYD SCOTT

TO CONSIDER a change in the elementary school arithmetic program is to consider an extremely complex problem. In addition to the important attention given the content of the program and its logical representation, children must be considered. The interaction of known and unknown attributes of children and their learning comprises an amorphous system of possibilities. While a great deal is known of children's developmental characteristics at the various elementary school ages and there is a consensus regarding certain features of children's learning, a vast area of uncertainty accompanies the framing of a program to fit the children. It is clear that the available research on human learning or on curriculum organization has not produced as yet a completely detailed and trustworthy model for elementary mathematics curriculum formulation. Hence, curriculum decisions in this area of consideration are often based upon intuition and the insight which derives from practical experience.

Similarly, teaching practice in today's elementary school classrooms reflects an uncertainty about the manner of learning arithmetic. In some classrooms one finds teachers as transmitters of knowledge, much in the manner of the early scribes and priests who collected number concepts and arranged them for transmission to apprentices. Pythagoras, for example, entered the priesthood in Egypt to learn the closely guarded secrets of the caste and later returned to Greece to establish classes of his own. The members of his classes were expected to memorize the concepts which he had acquired in order that they, in turn, could transmit them in due time. Some teachers today collect concepts and pass them along year by year to the children in their classes, mainly through the devices of extended practice and memorization.

Other teachers use questions as the medium of instruction and, at least to some extent, support what may be called the Socratic method. The questions and answers are designed to produce an integrated body of mathematical knowledge, but the interaction between most children and fundamental mathematical ideas is commonly sacrificed.

And then there are the teachers who resemble the schoolmaster described by Dickens and who follow what may be called the "Squeers method." This method consists mainly in the use of arithmetic as a device for creating mental discomfort among children. The amenability of the subject to increasing abstraction and complexity is exploited to the distaste of most sensitive youngsters. In these cases, as well as in many others for which examples could be drawn, there is a learning theory, albeit an individualized theory. Teaching proceeds according to the beliefs held by teachers as to what produces learning, and, to a large extent, the preparations of curricula are affected by the views of those directly associated with the preparation.

As indicated in the historical overview of curriculum change, some major trends in school arithmetic were dictated by prevailing views of learning. Certainly the mental discipline curriculum in the last part of the nineteenth century is an example of a program in concert with an accepted view of the nature of learning. Learning was viewed as a direct product of exercise of the mind. The mind was subjected to exercise just as the muscles were subjected to exercise by the weight lifter. As development of muscles proceeded, more weights were added, and as development of the mind proceeded, more arduous and difficult mental tasks were added. The textbooks which gave form to the program of this era included nothing but isolated and disconnected rules. They appealed to memory almost exclusively and neatly ignored the existence of reasoning powers in the mind of the learner.

The era of connectionism was also directly represented in the arithmetic program. In 1922, E. L. Thorndike had published his classic treatise on arithmetic learning entitled *The Psychology of Arithmetic*. While his "laws of learning" were often misunderstood and misrepresented, they nonetheless contributed to a practice of separating arithmetic into bits of learning. The appropriate teaching adjustment to the theory and to the dissected program was drill on the segments, facts and manipulations until the proper connections were established. Improper connections were to be avoided at all cost. In the final analysis, the program did produce computational skill, even though the application of the skill to problem solving was seldom made either within or without the school.

What may be called the meaning theory came into prominence in about 1935. This concept of learning arithmetic derived from the field theories of learning based upon Gestalt psychology and was diametrically opposed to the dissections which characterized the program aligned with connectionism. Learning was viewed as deriving from analysis of problems rather than from recalling information. The relatedness of the parts of an entire context was the center of the learning experience, rather than the isolated bits of which it was composed. A challenging problem was viewed as relatively unstructured and learning was viewed as the pursuit of some orderly structure through which the problem could be managed. When the relationship of the parts to the whole was rendered

clear, then insight was gained and learning had been achieved.

In general, the meaning theory continues to provide a basis for arithmetic program development. There remain open questions concerning the means through which insight is best achieved, and controversy probably will rage for some time to come. Thus, within the broad limits of the meaning theory there is room for many individual learning theories, each centering in a different point of view. It will be difficult always to know which "theory" is the absolute best in terms of societal goals and the characteristics of the learners, and it is often difficult to spot the most influential approach at a given moment.

However, within the current relevant literature some centers of curriculum influence may be noted. While these influences do not alter substantially the qualitative basis for detailed curriculum decisions, they seem to provide some common ground upon which general decisions may rest.

Notable among the current efforts which have been closely associated with modern curriculum development is the work of Professor Jean Piaget of Switzerland. Professor Piaget is perhaps best known as a developmental psychologist and his work with children has spanned a period of more than forty years. In his recent work, however, his interest in the intellectual and perceptual development of children has centered upon the relationship between thought activities and systems of logic and upon the growth of logical concepts in the individual. Of course, in this part of his activity he plays the role of the logician. Regardless of the particular classical identification of his work, curriculum projects are being increasingly affected by his theory and reported "experimental" results. At the present time, the most influential aspect of his studies upon new arithmetic curricula would seem to be the age-normative basis for intellectual growth which he has defined. In particular, he holds that a school child's ability to conceptualize may be seen to proceed through three rather distinct periods. The first may be designated the pre-operational period. This phase apparently continues from birth to about six years of age for most children. The pre-operational period is followed by the period of concrete operations which lasts until the child is about eleven years old. The third and last period defined by Piaget is designated the period of formal operations and this period extends through adulthood. While the transition points between periods have not been precisely fixed either by Piaget or by others who interpret or replicate his work, the ages of six and eleven may be regarded as rough guidelines.

The pre-operational period is characterized by a transition from the relatively random sensory-motor reactions of the infant to the pre-operational representations of the five-year-old. In general, this stage may be viewed as the stage of heavy reliance upon the senses and the gradual movement toward some symbolic representations for the sense impingements. There is little evidence of the development of a rational or structured conceptual framework.

The period of concrete operations is reserved for such organization of concrete experiences. Concepts are associated into cognitive structures called groupings, and these groupings serve as organization centers for the assimilation of the expanding experiences with the natural world. In this period the child is not able to deal effectively with ideas beyond his range of experience or beyond the reach of his senses. Objects serve to direct his thought, and interaction between the child and environmental objects provides the substance for his conceptual growth.

Piaget describes the period of formal operations as that period when the individual is capable of intellectual activity without the presence of objects. He is able to formulate ideas independent of corresponding sense encounters and he can perceive and analyze relationships among ideas. The learner in this period is attentive to logical development and interested in the orderly arrangement of facts and ideas. He finds it possible to extrapolate and operate beyond the immediately present ideas and he is in a position to extend the organization of knowledge.

Until very recently, there has been no substantial regard for the developmental stages defined by Piaget in the design of elementary school mathematics curricula. Today, however, there is a growing belief that human learning does proceed through some sequential defined stages and that these stages may be characterized by certain mental operations. The sequence of stages may well be invariant, as Piaget believes, though the rate of progress through the stages may be conditioned by certain factors under the control of the school. Furthermore, there is an increasing regard for a kind of analysis of thought activities based upon logical patterns. Piaget has promoted the belief that learning may be studied and classified into systems of operations; then these systems may be analyzed according to certain properties. Among the properties named by Piaget are: (1) composition—operations or suboperations may be combined into a new unit, (2) reversibility—combined units may be returned to original form and (3) associativity—the units may be grouped together in various ways, each with the same result. Such an approach brings a new dimension to the analysis of human thought. Without anticipating its ultimate worth in this important area of investigation, a new approach is somewhat akin to a breath of fresh air.

Another psychologist of influence in contemporary curriculum reform is Professor Jerome Bruner. In particular, his book entitled *The Process of Education*, which is a written summary of a major curriculum forum, has had a substantial impact upon program planning. Perhaps because the timing of publication of the volume was propitious, his treatment of the use of the structure of disciplines as the central notion in curriculum design was widely accepted and actively supported by major curriculum projects, especially those dealing with mathematics and science. While there were several operating curriculum groups involved in the formulation of programs which emphasized the unifying ideas in various subject matter areas, Bruner's convincing presentation of this point of view became a rallying point for these projects and they were soon joined by other groups impressed by the "structure" philosophy. Furthermore, the motivating aspects of inductive learning were stressed by Bruner, among others, and, despite an apparent conflict with the deductive nature of mathematics, induction and discovery became popular themes for program design. Thus, the selection and organization of program content and the approach to the material were conditioned by the perceived nature of children's learning.

The work of Z. P. Dienes has had some major effect upon the elementary school arithmetic program in transition, but the effect has been felt principally outside the United States. Only recently has his work drawn the attention of curriculum theorists in this country. While Professor Dienes may be best known for his development of mathematics teaching materials, his theoretical orientation has been effectively compatible with the Piaget and Bruner positions. Many designers of elementary mathematics curricula sought program improvement through a theoretical, abstract approach to the content of the mathematics. Dienes seems to follow the observations of Piaget, at least to the extent that the youngster in elementary school is seen to be at the concrete operations level of development. Dienes' development of materials was thus a consequence of his belief that concrete objects were necessary in mathematics learning during the first six or seven years of schooling. He demonstrated that there were different tendencies in thinking associated with motivation. He distinguished constructive thinking from analytic thinking and stressed the importance of constructivity, a process of synthesis of ideas through the manipulation of concrete materials. He saw the use of concrete objects in three sequentially ordered levels of experience. At the first level, the materials are used by children in an unstructured, undirected manner. According to Dienes, this is a necessary preliminary step before the materials can be organized or manipulated in an organized way. At the second level, the child's actions with the materials become directed toward some end. The materials are ordered and classified and symbolic representations, principally words, begin to be used in the production of ideas. At the third level, relationships and structural patterns are perceived by the child and insights are developed and strengthened. In all these levels, the interactions between children and materials are the crucial components of concept development. In essence, Dienes gives strong support to the view that constructive thinking must precede analytic thinking (Piaget's period of formal operations); otherwise there is nothing to analyze.

While the contributions of Piaget, Bruner and Dienes do not offer a unified or comprehensive theory of learning, they are illustrative and commonly cited bases for arithmetic curriculum decisions. It is interesting that there are apparent direct conflicts in the approaches of these theorists. For example, it would seem that Bruner would be satisfied if mention of learning readiness disappeared from the literature. The learning model of Piaget, on the other hand, is directly tied to the existence of readiness in the learner.

At the risk of oversimplifying the diverse psychological theories related to elementary school mathematics, the following detailed themes related to various views of human learning appeared to have received major attention:

1. The structure of mathematics should be stressed at all levels. Topics and relationships of endurance should be given concentrated attention.

2. Children are capable of learning more abstract and more complex concepts when the relationships between concepts is stressed.

3. Existing elementary arithmetic programs may be severely condensed because children are capable of learning concepts at much earlier ages than formerly thought.

4. Any concept may be taught a child of any age in some intellectually honest manner, if one is able to find the proper language for expressing the concept.

5. The inductive approach or the discovery method is logically productive and should enhance learning and retention.

6. The major objective of a program is the development of independent and creative thinking processes.

7. Human learning seems to pass through the stages of pre-operations, concrete operations and formal operations.

8. Growth of understanding is dependent upon concept exploration through challenging apparatus and concrete materials and cannot be restricted to mere symbolic manipulations.

9. Teaching mathematical skills is regarded as a tidying-up of concepts developed through discovery rather than as a step-by-step process for memorization.

10. Practical application of isolated concepts or systems of concepts, particularly those applications drawn from the natural sciences, are valuable to reinforcement and retention.

For many years American educators let the work of Jean Piaget pass unnoticed, partly because the original publications reporting his work were in French, and many Americans were unaware of his research, and partly because some of those who were aware of his work considered it somewhat interesting but of little value in helping plan learning experiences for children.

Piaget's books have now been translated, and attention is being given to his views. Both here and in England, Piagetian-type studies are being conducted and they confirm his findings. One result has been encouragement for providing children with activity-oriented learning experiences. A strong advocate of an activity-oriented program is Edith Biggs, Her Majesty's Inspector of Schools and Staff Inspector for Mathematics for the British Department of Education and Science. In this article, she discusses some of Piaget's tests and children's reactions to them. Miss Biggs helps you to gain a better understanding of why teachers are encouraged to provide children, particularly the beginner in mathematics, <u>with an activity-centered program.</u>

Research in Children's Method of Learning E.E. BIGGS

True or living learning originates from the child and indeed directly from some of his stronger interests and drives.

— Nathan Isaacs, Psychology, Piaget and Practice

IN THIS chapter we shall review the work of Piaget and others concerning the learning of mathematical concepts by young children. We shall then attempt to decide what influence their findings ought to have on our teaching of the early stages of mathematics.

Let us first turn to D. O. Hebb, of McGill University, for an unequivocal statement about the requirements of intellectual growth. 'There are two determinants of intellectual growth: a completely necessary innate potential and a completely necessary stimulating environment.'[1] If we accept this statement (and it is supported by the weight of prolonged research), our attention as teachers is directed once more to the importance of the environment. As we shall see, Piaget in his experimental methods sets us a pattern for use in planning our learning situations. In

his preface to *The Child's Conception of Number* he writes, 'Conversation with the child is more reliable and more fruitful when it is related to experience with adequate material, and when the child, instead of thinking in the void, is talking about actions he has just performed.'[2]

Piaget set himself the task of finding out, as accurately as possible, how the principles of conservation and of reversibility, as applied to numbers and to spatial thinking, develop in the minds of young children. These two principles are fundamental to all mathematical (and logical) thinking. For example, in the field of numbers, conservation means that the number of objects in a group remains the same however the objects are arranged (in a heap, in a long line, etc.). Or if we are considering quantities, a quantity of lemonade remains the same if it is poured, for example, from a shallow dish into a tall, narrow glass. The understanding of reversibility involves a realisation that reversing an action would result in a return to the original state of affairs.[3]

---

[1]*The Organisation of Behaviour*, p. 302. New York, 1949.

[2]*The Child's Conception of Number*, 1952. La Genèse du Nombre chez l'Enfant, Geneva, 1941.

[3]Not all operations are immediately reversible. When we let a bath of water drain away we cannot get the same water back again.

Piaget devised a variety of tests and tried these out on children of pre-school and primary school age.

Although the ages are always quoted in the records, it is the stages of learning to which Piaget draws attention. He was the first to discover that the formation of a concept takes far longer than had been supposed. His findings, and the stages of learning he postulates, are most easily understood in reference to one of his well known simple experiments.

This experiment was the third of a series concerned with one-to-one correspondence. In the test, the child was shown a set of seven egg-cups in a row and also a group of eggs (containing more than seven eggs). He was asked to take just enough eggs for the egg-cups. In Stage I (normally between the ages of four and five) one child made a row of the same length but containing too many eggs. He was then asked to put the eggs into the egg-cups to check his answer and was surprised to find there were too many eggs. The extra eggs were removed and the child agreed that now there were the same number of eggs and of egg-cups. But when the seven eggs were taken out and put in a heap in front of the egg-cups the child said that there were more egg-cups than eggs. It was clear from the similar responses of many children that, at this stage, children are not capable, by themselves, of making the one-to-one correspondence and that they would not have discovered it if the relations between the egg and its cup had not forced them to do so. As for the equivalence of the two sets (eggs and egg-cups), the child's answers were based entirely on a visual (perceptual) comparison of the length of the rows, even when one-to-one correspondence had been established by the nature of the materials.

In Stage II (normally between the ages of five and six) the child, of his own volition, took seven eggs to correspond to seven egg-cups and put the eggs in the cups. When the eggs were removed and spaced further apart, the child said there were more eggs than egg-cups. When asked if there would be the right number of eggs to put one egg back in each cup he did not know. Here the child created one-to-one correspondence for himself, but he no longer recognised the equivalence of the two sets once the configuration was changed.

In Stage III (normally between the ages of five-and-a-half and six-and-a-half) the child achieves 'operational correspondence and lasting equivalence.' Even when the eggs were spread out the child maintained that the number of eggs and egg-cups were the same, 'because they all go into the egg-cups.' It is only at this stage that reversibility is understood; that is, the child can reverse the thinking process and put the eggs back into the egg-cups in imagination. So the child has achieved full operational control of the concept.

Piaget has thus drawn attention to the fact that there are variations in kinds of thinking according to chronological or mental age. Of these kinds of thinking, Dr. E. A. Lunzer in *The Work of Piaget and its Relevance for the Teacher*[4] writes: 'The ability to carry out actions in our heads, actions of ordering and reordering, and of appreciating equivalences . . . is what Piaget calls operational reasoning. Such reasoning always involves systematic equivalences; for example, doing something (like adding) and then doing the opposite (like subtracting the same number) brings us back to where we began.'

. . . .

The importance Piaget placed on the use of the spoken word in his

---

[4]Unpublished manuscript. Manchester University.

experience with children raises the issue of the place of language in children's learning. In a carefully controlled piece of research work with a limited number of English children between the ages of 5.3 and 5.9 Mrs. J. Tough[5] investigated the contributions made by relevant experience and language to the formation of a number concept by five-year-old children.

Of the four groups considered, the group with whom the appropriate language was introduced at the same time as the experience made significant progress in the learning of the concept under consideration. Half the children in the group having experience without appropriate language had made some progress but in two control groups very little progress had been made. In Mrs. Tough's own words: 'Of the three situations explored, the basic concept is more efficiently formed when language and concrete experience appear together. For the schools this means the provision of good concrete experience together with active teacher-participation and the stimulation of a discussion.' Although this experiment involved a relatively small number of children the results are decisive and merit much further research. We are therefore left with the following three questions. Are we sufficiently aware of the concepts basic to later mathematical understanding? Do we provide the right kind of concrete experience during the early years? Do we provide at the same time language which helps efficient organisation of the experience?

This investigation shows the significance which one aspect of Piaget's work can have for teachers. What significance has Piaget's work

in general for us as teachers? Once more let us turn to the experts in this field for more specific guidance. Dr. Lunzer[6] writes: 'The principal field for the application of Piaget's methods and results in educational practice is that of curriculum and method.' Of children's understanding of number he writes that such understanding cannot be taught nor does it come by itself, independently of experience. It is the fact that number is an integral part of our daily lives which ensures that children do come to this understanding. 'This does not mean that there is nothing the teacher can do except wait for the dawn of understanding.' He can provide the kind of experience which will assist the child to move from intuitive to operational thinking. 'This (operational thinking) means activity, but activity in the sense of mental activity.' Not only must the experience provided be of the right sort; it must occur in a context in which the child is interested in the result. From this we can conclude (1) that we can promote understanding of mathematical concepts by providing experience of the right kind, (2) that the experience or activity provided is not an end in itself although it is planned to arouse interest; it is devised with the declared purpose of stimulating spontaneous discovery by the child.

Now if we want to plan the right kind of experience we must know (1) the mathematical concepts we want the children to learn, and (2) how children learn.

We shall turn our attention to the first problem in subsequent chapters. Piaget's methods help us with the second for he based his conclusions on his observation of young children. It is almost impossible for us as adults either to remember how we learnt mathematical concepts or to imagine ourselves

---

[5]*A study of the contributions made by relevant experience and language to the formation of a number concept of five-year-old children.* Unpublished thesis, 1963.

---

[6]*Op. cit.*

ignorant of them (imperfect though our knowledge may be). Therefore it is essential, if we want to discover how children learn, to plan learning situations for them and to observe what they do. It was by observing their actions, and by questioning them and listening to their answers, that Piaget discovered how the children were thinking and reasoning and learning.

Now let us see what a research worker in a different field has to say about Piaget's work. Dr. Z. P. Dienes relates Piaget's three stages of forming concepts to different types of learning situations. He calls the first the preliminary or play stage and writes: 'In order to make play possible, freedom to experiment is necessary.'[7] This stage is marked by an undirected and seemingly purposeless activity. The second stage is more directed and purposeful but there is no clear realisation of what is being sought. At this stage a certain degree of structured activity is desirable but, because children think in different ways, Dr. Dienes recommends the provision of a number of experiences of varying structure, all leading to the same concept. The third stage must provide the practice necessary for fixing the concept. He therefore refers to: (a) preliminary games, (b) structural games, and (c) practice games, but adds, 'Clearly a practice game for one concept can act as a preliminary game for a later concept. It is important, however, not to use practice games as preliminary games for the same concept, a common error in infants' schools.'

. . . .

With discovery methods in mind and encouraged by Piaget's experiments, let us create a dynamic

[7] *Building up Mathematics* by Z. P. Dienes, p. 39. Hutchinson, 1960.

definition for the learning of mathematics. To be brief we might content ourselves with: 'Mathematics is a discovery of relationships.' But if we (or the children we teach) have discovered such a relationship for ourselves we want to communicate the exciting discovery to others. We may first describe the discovery in words to a friend or teacher. Subsequently we may find a more effective way of expressing the relationship; for example, in numbers (as in arithmetic), in letters (as in algebra), by a diagram (as in geometry) or by a graph. Therefore a more comprehensive definition would be, 'Mathematics is a discovery of relationships and the expression of the relationship in symbolic (or abstract) form.' This is no static definition but implies action on the part of the learner, of whatever age and whatever ability. It is the fact that mathematical relationships can be discovered and communicated in such a variety of ways that puts mathematics within reach of children and adults of all abilities. In the following chapters we shall show how young children can learn mathematics by their own efforts and how we can plan the learning situations which will effect this. For this purpose we may summarise the conclusions derived from the research to which reference has been made in this chapter as follows:

1. Children learn mathematical concepts more slowly than we realised. They learn by their own activities.

2. Although children think and reason in different ways they all pass through certain stages depending on their chronological and mental ages and their experience.

3. We can accelerate their learning by providing suitable experiences, particularly if we introduce the appropriate language simultaneously.

4. Practice is necessary to fix a concept once it has been understood, therefore practice should follow, and not precede, discovery.

Reprinted from *Mathematics in Pri-mary Schools*, Curriculum Bulletin No. 1, Schools Council, London, England, 1965, pp. 5-9. Used by permission of the Controller of Her Brittanic Majesty's Stationery Office and the author.

Z. P. Dienes and E. W. Golding are other advocates of the activity-centered approach to learning. Their research and the materials they have developed have influenced mathematics programs tremendously. In the following article they help us envision the classroom setting in which active learning occurs. The role of the teacher, they point out, is not a passive one, but rather is active along with the children. ' After you read the article you should understand better how the teacher's role has changed from purveyor of rules and facts to one who guides children as they discover mathematics facts and relationships.

The Classroom Situation

Z. P. DIENES AND E. W. GOLDING

DRASTIC changes in the mathematics curriculum would not be possible if we were to retain the traditional classroom procedures and atmosphere at the same time. In fact, we hope that teachers will endeavour to change "a teaching situation" into "a learning situation." It must be emphasized that, with the kind of approach suggested here, far less "whole class teaching" will take place. Much of the work will be done by children working in small groups, or even individually. These groups can be formed by the teacher, or she may allow the children to form themselves into groups. They will work together quite happily, especially if the work is not spoiled for them by the creation of a reward-punishment system. Children are essentially interested in finding out new things about their world, and we do not have to spoil this interest by introducing compulsions or rewards for work well done. A smile from the teacher, or a pat on the back, is quite sufficient reward for a task well completed.

If we work in this way, the children will be encouraged to learn mathematics for its own sake, and not in order to excel or outdo their classmates in competition. Groups will form, will change in composition, and re-form, as some children learn more quickly than others. There will be a place for individual work, too, and there will be times when it will be more profitable for the whole class to work together. A case in point occurs in the study of sets. Sets are probably most satisfactorily introduced by considering the children in the class as possible members of any sets. In other words the universal set can, in the first place, be defined as the set of all the children in the class. At a later stage, too, equivalence games are most easily played by using the children themselves. When the question is asked, "Are there more chairs than children, or more children than chairs?" the children

will readily find out, if they are
allowed to do so, by trying to sit
on the chairs. If all the children
are able to sit down, one to a seat,
and there are some empty chairs,
then, of course, there are more
chairs than children—and nobody
needs to know the exact numbers of
children or chairs. In these situations the joint experience of the
class, or at any rate of a large
part of the class, will be benefi-
cial. So no hard and fast rules can
be laid down as to whether individual work, small group work, or whole
class work is the best way to handle
a situation. It must, in the last
resort, be left to the teacher to
choose what he feels is the best
approach in the situation in which
he finds himself. Very frequently,
when a new aspect is to be introduced, the class will be best taken
as a whole. This activity may not
last long, for it may be found that
progress has been so varied that the
next stage must be taken in groups—
and this may be so even before one
lesson has been completed.

An important part of learning
takes place by discussions among the
children. To illustrate this let us
take the case of a logical game,
with a Venn Diagram being completed
on the floor. If a child puts a
piece in the wrong place, it is much
less useful for the teacher to interfere than for another child to correct it. The two children can argue
the matter out on the same level,
and the child who thinks the piece
has been wrongly placed will usually
argue quite forcibly, while the other
child argues the point back again.
The rules of the game are quite simple enough for the truth to prevail
eventually in such an argument.
This is very good training, as it is
very much better to encourage children to appeal to the truth in a
situation than to appeal to the
authority of some person who is a
purveyor of truth, such as a teacher.
When children are encouraged to

discuss not only what they are doing
but also what they believe they
have discovered, quite naturally
there will be a certain amount of
noise in the classroom. However,
there is no need to allow excessive
noise to prevent learning from tak-
ing place or to interrupt the activities of other classes. The
teacher must realize that he is
still in charge, and must insist
that necessary noise be limited.
But, it is amazing how much noise
a child is able to support, while
yet doing a considerable amount of
delicate thinking. It is usually
the teacher who is "driven mad" by
the excessive amount of noise, and
not the children. On the other
hand, just as the teacher must get
used to a more noisy situation, the
children must learn to consider
others. We have found that, with
a little "give and take," this
problem is usually solved satisfactorily.

If the children learn best by
activity methods, and if discussion
will help such learning, the teacher
must adjust to the new situation;
while, if children are to learn in
the usual school situation with
other classes nearby, they must
limit the volume of noise that they
create.

In the implementation of a scheme
of learning such as described in
this handbook, there will be a
great amount of concrete material
to be handled by the children and
by the teacher. Taken in conjunction with group and individual work,
this calls for a considerable
amount of organization; if the
activities and the materials are
not properly organized there will
be chaos, loss of time, and poor
learning conditions. One way of
making sure that every child knows
exactly what to start with at the
beginning of a lesson is to put a
diagram on the blackboard, with
the names of children or groups
beside each section of the dia-

gram. Sketches are sometimes necessary because children cannot yet read instructions: thus we might use three interlocking circles for a Venn Diagram, or a quick sketch of some blocks to show an exchanging game. The materials, too, must have a definite place in the classroom, or in the corridor, where the children are able to reach them, so that, before the mathematics lesson, the teacher can simply ask certain responsible children to collect materials, put them where they will be needed, and distribute cards. At the end of the lesson, children may again be asked to check materials, pack and replace them tidily in the cupboards.

Once such an organization has been established there seems to be no trouble in getting the class started, but it certainly does need organizing; it will not happen by itself. Except at such times as when a new aspect is to be introduced, teachers will be well advised to "stagger" the changeover periods of the groups or of the individual children so that the beginning of a lesson sees most children continuing an activity of which they have some knowledge, while only a few must be introduced to something new. This, too, calls for considerable ability as an organizer.

It is not possible for a traditionally trained teacher to pass over to this kind of mathematics without a certain amount of heart-searching, and a consequent change in attitude. For example, the idea that truth is the authority, and not the teacher, is something rather difficult for some teachers to accept. Children themselves are accustomed simply to "ask the teacher." It is very tempting to interfere with children when they are making mistakes, and tell them how to do things when they don't know. It is quite difficult to stand by and watch a child fumbling away, not being able to solve a problem, when

all the teacher would have to do would be to say, "Look, put it over there," and it would be done. This, of course, would rob the child of the benefit arising from that particular learning situation in which he is expected to discover for himself what the solution is. By solving it for himself, he has the opportunity of fixing the solution in his mind very much more clearly and permanently than if the teacher merely tells him what to do.

In addition teachers should try to remember that the ways in which they think are not necessarily the ways in which the children think. In fact, child-thinking is very different from adult-thinking, and even different children seem to think problems out in different ways. There is no single way to solve a problem. Very often a child, given the opportunity, will suggest an avenue of attack for a problem which is not the avenue that the teacher himself would have chosen—in fact, the line of attack might seem to him to be entirely wrong. The best educational approach in such a case would have the teacher avoid saying, "That is wrong: do it this way," and have him join with the child in an investigation of what is entailed in the child's suggestion. A discussion, or a joint piece of discovery, could then follow, with the child's approach examined for what it is worth. If it is a good one, and if the child is intelligent enough to follow it up, he may convince the teacher. If this does not happen, and the child goes on fumbling and finding that the method is not particularly successful, then it will be time for the teacher to suggest that some other line of attack might be advisable.

It should not be thought, because it is suggested that children should not be unduly interfered with, that this implies that they should always be left entirely to their own devices. Occasional helpful suggestions from the teacher are a very necessary part of the learning process, but these should never take the form of commands. A child's mistake should not be pointed out to him in so many words, even though it be apparent to the teacher. The consequences of the mistakes should become apparent to the child. He must realise his result is absurd, and it will then be borne in on him that his approach was incorrect. It is very much better to discover one's own mistakes than to be told about them by someone else, and in the process it is found that more is learned about the structure of the problem. If the child is told, "No. It is wrong; you don't do it this way. Do it that way," he learns nothing about the problem, for he has not had any personal active experience of handling it.

Reprinted from *Learning Logic, Logical Games*, by Z. P. Dienes and E. W. Golding, pp. 10–14. New York, Herder and Herder, 1966. Used by permission.

Further Reading

Some of you will want to do additional reading about the theories of Bruner, Dienes, and Piaget and about the active approach to learning. Hopefully you will have the time as well as the desire. The following books are suggested.

Biggs, Edith E. *Mathematics for Younger Children*. New York: Citation Press, 1971. 68 pages.

Biggs, E. E., and MacLean, James R. *Freedom to Learn*. Don Mills, Ontario: Addison-Wesley Publishing Co. (Canada), 1969. 206 pages.

Brearley, Molly, and Hitchfield, Elizabeth. *A Guide to Reading Piaget*. New York: Schocken Books, 1966. 171 pages.

Bruner, Jerome S. *The Process of Education*. New York: Vintage Books, 1960. 97 pages.

_____. *Toward a Theory of Instruction*. Cambridge, Mass.: The Belknap Press of Harvard University Press, 1966. 176 pages.

Copeland, Richard W. *How Children Learn Mathematics: Teaching Implications of Piaget's Research*. New York: The Macmillan Co., 1970. 310 pages.

Dienes, Z. P. *Building Up Mathematics*. London: Hutchinson Educational, 1960. 124 pages.

_____. *The Power of Mathematics*. London: Hutchinson Educational, 1964. 176 pages.

Isaacs, Nathan. *New Light on Children's Ideas of Number: The Work of Professor Piaget*. London: Ward Lock Educational Company, 1960. 41 pages.

Kidd, Kenneth P.; Myers, Shirley S.; and Cilley, David M. *The Laboratory Approach to Mathematics*. Chicago: Science Research Associates, 1970. 282 pages.

Lamons, William E. *Learning and the Nature of Mathematics*. Chicago: Science Research Associates, 1972. 236 pages.

Lovell, Kenneth. *The Growth of Understanding in Mathematics: Kindergarten through Grade Three*. New York: Holt, Rinehart and Winston, 1971. 204 pages.

Morrow, Casey, and Morrow, Liza. *Children Come First*. New York: Harper & Row, Publishers, 1971. 306 pages.

National Council of Teachers of Mathematics. *Piagetian Cognitive-Development Research and Mathematical Education*. Washington, D.C.: National Council of Teachers of Mathematics, 1971. 243 pages.

Schminke, C. W., and Arnold, William R. *Mathematics Is a Verb*. Hinsdale, Ill.: Dryden Press, 1971. 366 pages.

Self-Evaluation Checklist

The final activity for this chapter is the checklist that appears on the following pages. After you mark the checklist get a scope-and-sequence chart for one of the mathematics series listed in Appendix A. These charts are found in some teacher's guides. Your instructor may have a large chart from one of the publishers that he will let you use. Find the column on the chart for the grade level of your choice and compare the topics listed there with your yes and no answers on the checklist. Do any of the topics you see listed surprise you?

If you have many checks in the "I don't understand it at all" and "I understand it to some extent" columns, you will need to improve your understanding of the mathematics included in elementary school programs. You should consult with your instructor to see what you can do.

SELF-EVALUATION CHECKLIST

Name_____

Date_____

Instructor_____

Directions: Assume that you are to begin teaching at the grade level of
your choice in the morning. Indicate in the space provided
the grade level(s) for which you are preparing to teach.
Following that, you will find a number of mathematics topics.
For each topic, you are to make two responses. One, tell
whether or not you believe the topic is one which you expect
to find taught at the grade level(s) of your choice. Two,
indicate how adequate you believe your present *knowledge of
the topic* is for teaching that topic at *any* grade from kindergarten through grade six. (It is assumed that you do not
yet know of materials and procedures for teaching these topics; respond only in terms of how well you presently understand each topic.)

Grade level(s)_____

Mathematics topics:

Taught at grade levels of my choice:		Adequacy of my understanding for teaching at any grade level—kindergarten through six:		
		I don't understand it at all.	I understand it to some extent.	I have a good understanding of it.
Yes	No			
1. *Prime numbers*				
⎯⎯	⎯⎯	⎯⎯	⎯⎯	⎯⎯
2. *Factors and factoring*				
⎯⎯	⎯⎯	⎯⎯	⎯⎯	⎯⎯
3. *Numeration systems having bases other than ten*				
⎯⎯	⎯⎯	⎯⎯	⎯⎯	⎯⎯
4. *Clock arithmetic (modular systems)*				
⎯⎯	⎯⎯	⎯⎯	⎯⎯	⎯⎯
5. *"Casting out nines"*				
⎯⎯	⎯⎯	⎯⎯	⎯⎯	⎯⎯
6. *Reciprocals & their uses*				
⎯⎯	⎯⎯	⎯⎯	⎯⎯	⎯⎯

Mathematics topics: *continued*

Taught at grade levels of my choice:		Adequacy of my understanding for teaching at any grade level—kindergarten through six:		
Yes	No	I don't understand it at all.	I understand it to some extent.	I have a good understanding of it.
7. Commutative principle for addition				
———	———	———	———	———
8. Associative principle for addition				
———	———	———	———	———
9. Commutative principle for multiplication				
———	———	———	———	———
10. Associative principle for multiplication				
———	———	———	———	———
11. Distributive principle (multiplication over addition)				
———	———	———	———	———
12. Sets and set theory				
———	———	———	———	———
13. Nonmetric geometry— closed, not closed curves				
———	———	———	———	———
14. Nonmetric geometry— points, lines, and plane and closed-surface figures				
———	———	———	———	———
15. Nonmetric geometry— congruency and symmetry				
———	———	———	———	———
16. Metric geometry—English system—i.e., inches, feet, pints, quarts, etc.				
———	———	———	———	———
17. Metric geometry— metric system				
———	———	———	———	———

Mathematics topics: *continued*

	Taught at grade levels of my choice:		Adequacy of my understanding for teaching at any grade level—kindergarten through six:		
	Yes	No	I don't understand it at all.	I understand it to some extent.	I have a good understanding of it.
18. *Logic*	____	____	____	____	____
19. *Statistics and probability*	____	____	____	____	____
20. *Functions*	____	____	____	____	____

2
Using Performance Objectives

A SET of attribute materials consisting of letters enclosed in squares and identification cards is printed at the end of this chapter. Remove this page from your manual and cut out the letter squares and identification cards. In addition to the attribute materials you will need three loops made by tying together the ends of each of three six-foot lengths of string.

Letter squares, like all sets of attribute materials, are designed to help children develop their abilities to classify members of sets and to discover class relationships. These abilities, which have been described as fundamental to mathematics and even to life itself, develop over time, beginning early in school as children work with materials such as letter squares or teacher-prepared collections of items such as old buttons or used postage stamps.

Initially children should have time for free exploration with their materials. During this "free play" they acquire the ability to describe each piece within the set. Eventually an agreed upon, accurate description of the set must be made. Write a statement which you believe accurately describes the letter squares.

Following the introductory stage, children can be asked to separate the set into subsets. With most sets there are a number of possible ways of separation. It is important that children recognize this as they work with objects they can manipulate. When they work with objects they build foundations for understanding how to classify elements within sets of numbers or sets of geometric points and how to solve problems in logic, where they deal with abstract ideas rather than objects.

Describe at least three different subsets into which the set of letter squares can be separated.

In addition to using attribute materials for classification activities and separation into subsets, there are many games children can play to develop logical thinking. Work with one or two classmates to devise at least one game using letter squares. Describe your game.

TUESday 21

You have explored ways of using letter squares and have discussed with classmates how these squares can be used to enhance your understanding of certain concepts and to develop skill in classifying and ordering elements of sets. Keeping in mind that the author's goal in writing this manual is to help you become an effective teacher of elementary school mathematics, what reasons can you give for having been asked to work with these materials now rather than later? In other words, what objectives do you think you were to attain as a result of your explorations and discussions? Write a statement for each objective that occurs to you at this time. (Three objectives are listed on the next page, but try not to peek at them just yet.)

Here are three objectives (reasons) for using letter squares:

1. The learner will *become acquainted* with the letter squares' attributes and their values.

2. The learner will *know* the role of letter squares (or any other attribute materials) in a modern mathematics program.

3. The learner will *recognize* the understandings about sets and subsets which can be developed through the use of letter squares.

Compare these objectives with the ones you wrote. Did you think of some of the same objectives?

Now write a paragraph giving your opinion about the adequacy of each of these statements—how well it states the objective connected with it. Be sure to include reasons for your opinions.

If your opinion about the way these objectives are stated is favorable, you should take another look at them and reconsider. They are not really good statements.

Why are these poor statements of objectives? They are poor because they are too general; they are vague and imprecise. After you have read each one you still do not know what a person can do to show that he has achieved the objective. How does a person who *becomes acquainted* with the letter squares' attributes and their values, *knows* their role in the mathematics program, and *recognizes* understandings developed while using them behave to show that he has *become acquainted*, that he *knows* and *recognizes*?

We can rewrite these statements so that they become useful objectives, but first we need a clear understanding of what an objective is. *An objective is a concise statement of what a learner will be able to do as a result of an educational experience.* When defined in this manner an objective is called a *performance*, or *behavioral*, *objective*. The key phrase in the definition is "*what a learner will be able to do*." Mager says,

> Until you describe what the learner will be DOING when demonstrating that he "understands" or "appreciates," you have described very little at all. Thus, the statement that communicates best will be one that describes the terminal behavior of the learner well enough to preclude misinterpretation.[1]

An important task in writing objectives is to specify as precisely as possible what the learner will be able to do as a result of a learning experience. Because some verbs describe behavior vaguely, it is necessary to choose verbs carefully. You must select those which describe behavior precisely. In the following list underline the verbs you believe are subject to the fewest misinterpretations.

identifies	values	ensures	demonstrates
describes	lists	likes	selects
engages in	fancies	contrasts	organizes
learns	accepts	solves	states a rule

The verbs in the list which indicate forms of observable behavior are *identifies*, *describes*, *lists*, *contrasts*, *solves*, *demonstrates*, *selects*, *organizes*, and *states a rule*.

The objectives for working with the letter squares can be improved by substituting some of the verbs from the list for those in the original statements. "The learner will *become acquainted* with the letter squares' attributes and their values" can be changed to "The learner will *identify* the attributes of the letter squares and *describe* their values." It is difficult to judge whether a person has *become acquainted* with the letter squares, but it is quite easy to determine if he can *identify* their attributes and *describe* each attribute's values. The identification and description can be oral or written. Either way, the completeness and correctness of the learner's responses can be judged by comparing them with an existing list of attributes and description of their values. The

---

[1]Robert R. Mager, *Preparing Instructional Objectives* (Belmont, Calif.: Fearon Publishers, 1962), p. 11. (Emphasis in original.)

objective is improved by substituting the verbs *identify* and *describe* for *become acquainted.*

Rewrite the other two objectives, using verbs from the list, so that each includes a form of observable behavior.

In addition to the condition that objectives be stated in terms of observable behavior, two other conditions are frequently included: (1) the conditions under which the learner will operate to attain and demonstrate mastery of the objective and (2) the level or degree of proficiency he is expected to achieve. When these conditions are added the first objective might become "*Given a maximum of one hour of individual or small-group exploratory activities using letter squares and a class discussion of the squares and their uses*, the learner will identify *three significant* attributes of the squares and will describe each attribute's values." The first condition is given in the first part of the objective. We now know that the learner will be given up to one hour for exploratory activities followed by a class discussion of unspecified length before he is expected to identify the attributes and describe their values. We also know that there are three significant attributes to be identified.

Whether either or both of these conditions is included in the objective depends upon the degree to which their inclusion improves communication of the writer's instructional intent. These conditions should be included when they are necessary to provide a learning situation essentially the same as the one intended by the writer and then to provide a basis for judging if the learner has attained the objective.[2]

---

[2]For additional information about these conditions and their applications to writing objectives, see chapters 5 and 6 in Mager, *Preparing Instructional Objectives.*

Read the other two objectives as you have rewritten them and decide whether communication of your instructional intent for each can be improved by including either or both of these conditions. If you believe they can be improved, rewrite them a second time.

Using Performance Objectives in the Classroom

The use of performance objectives to improve instruction has been recommended for at least a decade, but few mathematics textbook series use them in their teacher's guides. Most guides do include goals for each chapter or unit and objectives for each lesson, but these are usually stated in general rather than in performance terms.

One of the goals for chapter 1 of the fourth-grade book in a popular series is "To develop concepts relating to sets and subsets."[3] Within the chapter, one lesson has this objective, which is also called a goal: "To develop the idea that a set can be shown by listing its members or by describing them."[4] Because this is one of the concepts referred to in the goal, it would be helpful to state the objective in a way that tells what the learner does when he shows sets by listing their members or describing them. One way to do this is to rewrite the objective: "Given five sets, each containing six or fewer familiar objects, the learner will identify each set in two ways: (1) by listing the members and (2) by describing the members." Now the objective is stated so that the learner's terminal behavior is clearly described. With this objective in mind, we can select

---

[3]Duncan, Capps, Dolciani, Quast, and Zweng, *Modern School Mathematics: Structure and Use*, teacher's annotated ed., Book V, p. 16. Copyright © 1967 by Houghton Mifflin Company. Reprinted by permission.

[4]*Ibid.*, p. 22.

activities which will help the student learn to use both the roster and descriptive methods of showing sets. At the same time we have established an acceptable level of achievement, so we can determine whether or not a student has attained the objective.

The following examples of chapter goals and lesson objectives are from teacher's annotated editions of the Houghton Mifflin Company's series, *Modern School Mathematics: Structure and Use*.[5] The book number is given first, followed by a chapter goal and the page on which the goal is found. Each goal is followed by one or more lesson goals (objectives). You are to rewrite each lesson goal so that it is stated as a performance objective, using the spaces at right for your statements.

---

[5]Duncan, Capps, Dolciani, Quast, and Zweng, *Modern School Mathematics: Structure and Use*, teacher's annotated ed., Books 1-6. Copyright © 1967 by Houghton Mifflin Company. Reprinted by permission.

Rewrite each lesson goal as a performance objective

BOOK 1: *To introduce the language and symbolism of addition and subtraction (p. 76).*
To use the frame in equations such as $1 + \square = 3$ (p. 88).
To introduce the minus sign and the subtraction equation (p. 98).
BOOK 2: *To develop the associative property of addition (p. 54).*
To introduce addition with three addends and the associative property of addition (p. 58).
BOOK 3: *To develop the multiplication-division facts with 2, 3, 4, and 5 as factors (p. 152).*
To introduce the concept of multiplication as repeated addition (p. 154).
To emphasize the concept that multiplication and division are opposite (inverse) operations (p. 158).
BOOK 4: *To introduce some ideas relating to logic (p. 264).*
To develop the meaning of "all," "some," or "none" (p. 288).
To begin to develop the concept of if-then thinking through the use of subsets (p. 290).

BOOK 5: *To present the concepts of common factors and multiples, greatest common factor and the least common multiple (p. 202).*
To introduce and develop the concept of the greatest common factor of two numbers (p. 206).
To introduce the concepts of common multiples and least common multiples (p. 210).
To introduce and develop the concept of prime numbers (p. 212).
BOOK 6: *To reinforce the formulas for naming measures of areas and volumes (p. 320).*
To review measurement of line segments, angles, regions, and space (p. 324).
To reinforce the use of equations for naming volumes (p. 326).

As a concluding activity, you are to write performance objectives for a chapter or unit from a book in one of the mathematics series listed in Appendix A. Select the book for the grade level of your choice. Choose a chapter and read it and information about it given in the teacher's guide. When you have determined the objectives of the chapter, write each in performance terms. Have a classmate read and evaluate your objectives to determine how well each communicates your instructional intent.

List your objectives on paper.

A	E	O	U
A	**E**	**O**	**U**
A	**E**	**O**	**U**

Large	a	e	o	u
Small				
White	**a**	**e**	**o**	**u**
Gray				
Black	**a**	**e**	**o**	**u**
A E O				

U

3
Whole Numbers

Teacher-Directed Activities

CHILDREN spend more of the time devoted to mathematics on experiences with whole numbers than on any other single topic. They must understand whole numbers and master operations with them if they are to develop proficiency in mathematics. Experiences with addition and subtraction begin early in each child's school career, while work with multiplication and division generally comes a year or two later.

Because experiences with whole numbers begin early, teacher-directed activities form a significant part of the work. Teacher-led investigation involving manipulative devices enable children to develop an understanding of the whole number system and the meanings of the operations. Both commercial materials and materials made by teachers or children are used. As you complete the experiences for this chapter you will become acquainted with the abacus and beansticks as means of making whole numbers meaningful to children. You will also learn how children can interpret operations with whole numbers, using these and other simple devices and techniques. At the *Objective* conclusion of these experiences you will be able to:

1. Use an abacus and beansticks to illustrate the meaning of numbers greater than ten written in the Hindu-Arabic numeration system.

2. Express numbers using Hindu-Arabic numerals in their simplest expanded forms and three additional expanded forms.

3. Use an abacus and beansticks to illustrate addition and subtraction algorithms using the Hindu-Arabic numeration system.

4. Use an abacus to represent numbers expressed in base five and base eight numeration systems; be able to write expanded notation forms for numerals in these systems; and use addition and subtraction algorithms involving numbers expressed in bases five and eight.

5. Demonstrate with appropriate learning aids the repeated addition, array, and Cartesian (cross) product interpretations of multiplication with whole numbers.

6. Create word problems that illustrate both partitive and measurement situations for division.

7. Use the number line and pasteboard disks (or similar markers) to illustrate multiplication and division situations.

8. Explain the repeated subtraction algorithm for division.

The Hindu-Arabic Numeration System

The Hindu-Arabic numeration system originated in India well over a thousand years ago, and refinements were made over several hundred years. Gradually knowledge of the system spread to Europe, where the Roman numeration system was used, and to other parts of the world. Finally the superiority of the Hindu-Arabic system was acknowledged, and its use increased, whereas that of other systems diminished. Today the Hindu-Arabic system is used throughout the world, and although different languages contain different words to name numbers, numbers have the same meaning everywhere and are identified by the same symbols, or numeral forms.

The Abacus and Beansticks

Children must thoroughly understand the Hindu-Arabic system if they are to succeed in mathematics. As you engage in the following activities you will become acquainted with two commonly used devices for making the system and number operations meaningful to children—the abacus and beansticks. The abacus has a long history as a computing device. It has been adapted for today's classroom to illustrate the meaning of numbers when expressed in the Hindu-Arabic and nondecimal systems and to show how these systems are used for performing number operations, particularly addition and subtraction. Beansticks have recently been introduced for illustrating the meanings of numbers and numeration systems.[1]

---

[1]Beryl S. Cochran, *An Approach to Place Value Using Beans and Beansticks*

The following activities introduce you to the abacus and beansticks. You will need about a quarter cup of small dried beans, fifty or so popsicle or coffee stirrer sticks, and white glue. Also, remove the place value grouping boxes and abacus pages from your manual.

The Abacus

1. Form a cup with one hand and pour a small quantity of beans into it. Count the beans into sets of ten each. Put each set of ten beans in one of the boxes in the base section of the place value grouping boxes. If you fill all the boxes in the base section, remove the beans from these boxes and put them in the base times base box. Continue "boxing" the beans by putting sets of ten into the base boxes until fewer than ten remain. (If you fill all the base boxes a second time, remove the beans and put them beside the base times base box.) Put the remaining beans in the ones boxes, a bean to a box. Leave them there and read on.

2. Use additional beans to represent on the abacus the number of beans you put in your hand. Beginning at the right, place one bean on the line (rod) for each bean in the ones boxes. On the next rod, place one bean for each set of ten beans in the base boxes. Finally, put one bean on the middle rod for each set of one hundred beans in or beside the base times base box. Have a classmate tell you how many beans you poured into your hand by saying the number represented on your abacus.

3. Repeat this activity several times, using both larger and smaller handfuls of beans until you are thoroughly familiar with the processes of grouping beans by tens and representing numbers on an abacus.

([Box 1176], Weston, Conn. [06880]: Materials for Learning, 1970); and George Arbogast, *Beanstick Arithmetic* (Los Angeles: Division of Instructional Planning and Services, Los Angeles City Schools, 1969).

Beansticks

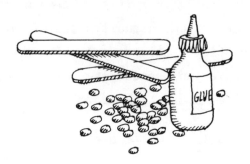

1. Make a set of beansticks, using dried beans, wooden sticks, and glue. There is no standard set of sticks—the size of a set varies with its uses. You will find a set such as the one illustrated below useful.

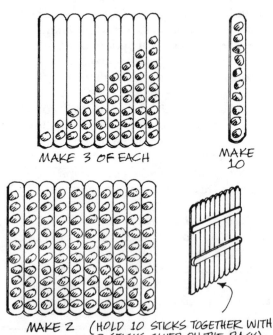

MAKE 3 OF EACH

MAKE 10

MAKE 2 (HOLD 10 STICKS TOGETHER WITH 2 STICKS GLUED ON THE BACK)

2. Select a partner with whom to work as you complete the introductory work with the beansticks and continue working with the abacus. On a slip of paper, write the numerals for five numbers, each smaller than five hundred; exchange your list for your partner's. Use your beansticks and the hundreds squares of your partner, if necessary, to represent each number named on your partner's list. At the same time, represent each number with beans on your abacus. Discuss with your partner any questions which arise about how the numbers are represented with either device.

Your understanding of the Hindu-Arabic numeration system will be extended as you and your partner work with your abacuses and beansticks to learn some expanded notation forms. Use the numbers named below for the following sequence of activities.

(a) 42   (b) 69   (c) 109

(d) 428   (e) 356   (f) 130

---

1. Each of these numbers is expressed in its common, or standard, form. To learn to express numbers in expanded numeral forms, study the abacus and beansticks as you use them to represent numbers. Represent 342 with each of these devices. With the abacus you should have two beans on the ones rod, four beans on the tens rod, and three beans on the hundreds rod. With beansticks you should have a stick containing two beans on the right, four tens sticks in the middle, and three hundreds squares on the left. In base ten there are ones, tens, and hundreds places, respectively, from right to left. With this in mind, 342 is rewritten in simple expanded form as "3 hundreds + 4 tens + 2 ones." (Sometimes

the word ones *is omitted, giving "3 hundreds + 4 tens + 2"). Rename each of the numbers named above in its simplest expanded form. (Your responses to this and the other exercises in this chapter should be written on your response sheet, which begins on page 73.)*

2. Another way to represent a number in an expanded form is with numerals alone rather than with numerals and words—for example, 342 = 300 + 40 + 2. Rename each of the numbers using this form.

3. Still another way to express numbers using expanded notation is with a multiplication form. The number 342 is then expressed as (3 × 100) + (4 × 10) + 2. Rename

each of the numbers using this form.

4. The final form that will be considered is one using exponents in the multiplication form. It is used most often when expressing large numbers. The number 342 is expressed as $(3 \times 10^2) + (4 \times 10^1) + (2 \times 10^0)$. Rename the numbers in (c) through (f) using this form.

5. Beginning with the simplest one, use each of the four forms to express the number 452,061.

6. Look through each book of one of the mathematics textbook series listed in Appendix A for uses, if any, of each of these forms. Describe briefly how expanded notation is used beginning in grade one and continuing through grade six.

Nondecimal Numeration Systems

Activities featuring work with nondecimal numeration systems are included in many of today's mathematics programs. Nondecimal systems are not included merely for the sake of making a program look modern. Rather, they are included because work with them helps children strengthen their understanding of place value systems, including the Hindu-Arabic system. As children engage in activities dealing with bases other than ten, they have frequent opportunities to make comparisons between the nondecimal systems and the Hindu-Arabic system. Through activities and discussions afterward, children learn to recognize the characteristics common to all place value systems and to make generalizations about them.

These activities are designed to enhance your understanding of place value systems, including the Hindu-Arabic. At the same time you will learn about activities that are appropriate for children's study of bases other than ten. You will need your container of beans, place value grouping boxes, and abacus.

BASE FIVE

1. Form a cup with one of your hands and pour a small quantity of beans into it. Count the beans into

sets of five each. If you have fewer than five sets put them a set at a time in the base boxes of your place value grouping boxes. The remaining beans will go into the ones boxes, a bean to a box. If you have five or more sets, combine them into sets of five times five beans. If there is only one such set, put it in the base times base box. If there are more than one, put the additional set(s) beside the base times base box. The remaining sets of five and the sin-

gle beans will be placed in the base and ones *boxes*. Leave the beans in the boxes and read on.

2. *Because the abacus is man-made, you can change yours to accommodate any base. For previous activities you have used it as a base ten recording device. Now you will use it as a base five recording device. Put beans on it to represent the grouping of beans in your place value grouping boxes. Complete the abacus pictured on your response sheet to show how yours looks.*

3. *The base five numeral that tells the number of beans you poured into your hand has a ones place, in-dicated by the first rod on the right of your abacus, a base place, indi-cated by the rod to the left of the ones rod, and, perhaps, a base times base place, indicated by the middle rod on your abacus. (This number is also represented in your place value grouping boxes by the sets of beans in the ones boxes, base boxes, and base times base boxes.) Write this numeral on your response sheet.*

4. *Repeat the process using larger and smaller handfuls of beans until you are familiar with groupings in base five, representing numbers on a base five abacus, and writing numerals in base five. Record your numerals on your response sheet.*

BASE EIGHT

5. *Pour out another small handful of beans. This time count them into sets of eight. If there are fewer than eight, put each set in one of the base boxes and the remaining beans in the ones boxes, one bean to a box. If there are eight or more sets, combine eight sets for the base times base box, then distribute the sets of eight and the single beans.*

6. *Your abacus is now a base eight device. Use it to show in this base the number of beans you poured into your hand. Complete a picture of the abacus and write the*

numeral on your response sheet.

7. *Again, repeat the process using larger and smaller amounts of beans. Record the numerals on your response sheet.*

Writing base five and eight numer-als in their expanded forms and then comparing these forms with each other and with those for base ten will highlight the common character-istics of all place value systems.

1. *Complete the blanks in the expanded forms that follow, using your base five numeral from Exercise 3 on this page.*

__twenty-five(s)+ __five(s)+ __one(s)

___ + ___ + ___

___ × (5 × 5) + ___ × (5) + ___

___ × (5^2) + ___ × (5^1) + ___ × (5^0)

(5 is used to express the base in these expanded forms to emphasize that this is a base five system. The numeral 5 is not a part of the system; 10 is the numeral for the number 5. 10 can be substituted for 5 in the expanded forms used here.) Write your base five numerals from Exercise 4, on this page, in the ex-panded forms on your response sheet.

2. *Complete the blanks in the expanded forms that follow, using your base eight numeral from Exer-cise 6 on this page*

__sixty-four(s)+ __eight(s)+ __one(s)

___ + ___ + ___

___ × (8 × 8) + ___ × (8) + ___

___ × (8^2) + ___ × (8^1) + ___ × (8^0)

(8 is used in the same manner and for the same reasons as 5 is used above.) Write your base eight numerals from Exercise 7, on this page, in the expanded form on your response sheet.

*3. *Sets of beansticks for base*

---

*Starred activities are optional. You may choose to do them to help you better understand the topic being considered or to practice before using them with children.

five and base eight can be used for the same purposes and in the same ways as sets for base ten. Make a set for base five or base eight. Repeat the base five and base eight activities (Exercises 1-7) above, substituting beansticks for the abacus.

4. By now you should be aware of certain characteristics that are common to the three numeration systems you have been studying. One is that they are all place value systems. Use your abacus, beansticks, and written responses to the exercises to identify other common characteristics. List these on your response sheet.

5. Examine the books in one of the elementary mathematics textbook series listed in Appendix A to see what, if any, work with bases other than ten is included. What materials for children to work with are recommended in teacher's manuals for the series? Can you adopt the abacus and beansticks to use with the textbook material? If so, in what ways?

As you perform the activities in this book you will come upon MATHEMATICS CAN BE FUN pages from time to time. These pages introduce you to recreational aspects of mathematics—puzzles, tricks, brainteasers, games, and so on. The activities on these pages are FUN to do. The MATHEMATICS CAN BE FUN pages can form the nucleus of a collection of recreational activities that you should assemble and keep on file.

Mathematics Can Be Fun

HIDDEN VOCABULARY PUZZLE

There are at least 85 mathematics words hidden in this puzzle. They are written forward and backward across a line of letters, up and down a column of letters, and down and up along a diagonal line of letters. How many can you find?

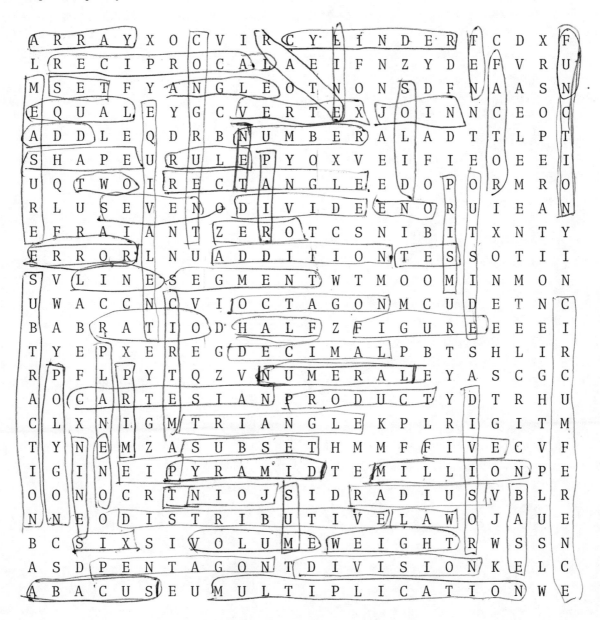

MAKE YOUR OWN PUZZLE

Use the grid on this page to make your own hidden vocabulary puzzle.
A puzzle for children in the elementary school should be simpler than the
one given here, although mature sixth-graders can find most of the words
hidden in it. For second- and third-grade classes you will want no more
than twelve to fourteen letters across and down. For fourth-, fifth-, and
sixth-grade classes, sixteen to twenty letters each way are sufficient.
Reduce the size of the grid, if necessary, before you begin your puzzle.
First list the words you want to include in your puzzle. Then fill
in consecutive squares across, down, and diagonally with the letters from
these words. You may find that you cannot include all the words from your
list, but by juggling them around you will get most of them in. To complete the puzzle, fill in the remaining squares, using letters at random.

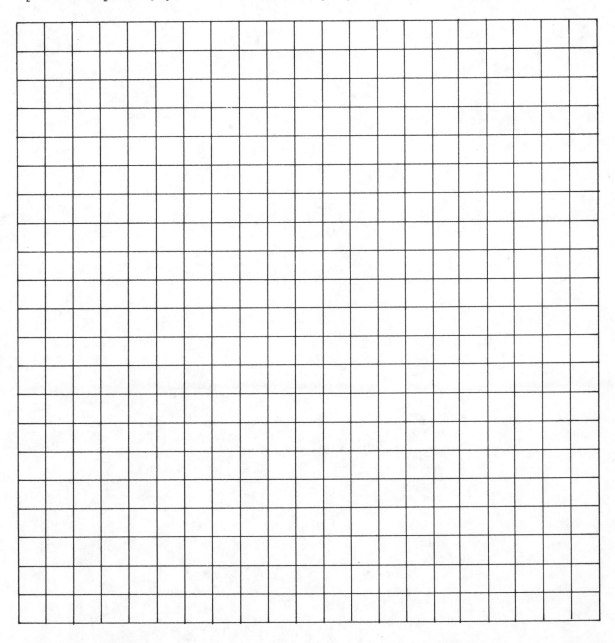

Four Operations on Numbers

There are four operations on numbers to which we devote a significant amount of time in the elementary school mathematics program: addition, subtraction, multiplication, and division. Activities dealing with addition and subtraction are included in this section; those dealing with multiplication and division are in the following section.

ADDITION AND SUBTRACTION

Addition can be described as the mathematical operation that indicates what takes place when the union of two or more disjoint sets is formed. Primary children should have numerous opportunities to join sets as they learn the meaning of this operation.

Later beansticks and the abacus (as well as other place value devices) can be used by children as they consider addition involving numbers too large to be represented conveniently with disks, blocks, and similar counting aids. These devices help children understand the conventional addition algorithm.

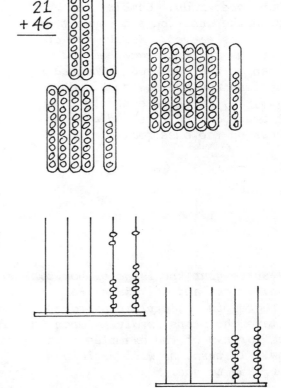

1. Use beansticks to illustrate the addition at right. First represent each addend with bean-sticks. Count the number of beans on the two ones sticks. Exchange these sticks for the 7 stick. Put the tens sticks together at the left of the 7 stick. The sum is the number of beans on the combined set of tens and ones sticks.

$$\begin{array}{r} 21 \\ +\,46 \end{array}$$

The same addition can be illustrated on the abacus. Represent 46 beans at the botton of the tens and ones rods; represent 21 with beans above those already in place. Join the beans on the ones rod; then join those on the tens rod. The sum is now represented by the six beans on the tens rod and the seven on the ones rod.

2. With a partner repeat the process with beansticks and the abacus for the following additions. Share the work as you and your partner explain to each other the steps using each device.

(a) 62
   +34

(b) 17
   +32

(c) 143
   +245

(d) 362
   +126

3. *Regrouping, or "carrying," for addition is illustrated with beansticks and abacus. First represent the two addends with beansticks. Count the number of beans on the two ones sticks. Since the total is eleven, exchange the 6 and 5 sticks for a 10 stick and a 1 stick. Combine all the tens sticks and put them to the left of the ones sticks. Determine the answer by counting the tens sticks and the beans on the ones stick.*

$$\begin{array}{r} 36 \\ +45 \\ \hline \end{array}$$

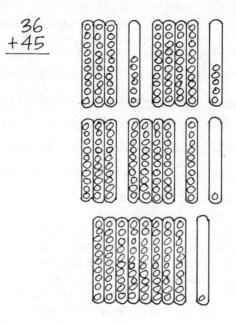

Now turn to your abacus. Represent each addend with beans on the tens and ones rods. Combine the beans on the ones rod and count them. The total is eleven. Remove ten of these beans and exchange them for one bean on the tens rod. The beans on the tens rod are now combined. The sum, 81, is represented by the eight beans on the tens rod and the one bean on the ones rod.

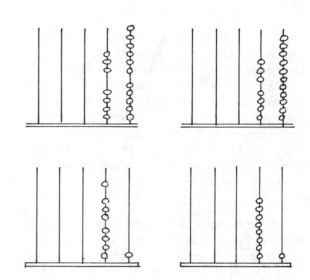

4. *Share your knowledge of how to use beansticks and the abacus to show regrouping by explaining to a classmate the steps involving each device for two of the examples that follow. In turn, he will explain two of them to you.*

(a) 63   (b) 56   (c) 237   (d) 196
   +28   +38   +181   +147

Subtraction is the inverse operation of addition. That is, subtraction undoes what is done by addition. It is the mathematical operation that indicates what takes place when a set *is separated into two subsets, when a subset is removed from a set, or when two sets are compared to determine which is larger or smaller.*

There is more than one way to perform subtraction in the algorithm form.[2] The decomposition, or "take-away," method of subtraction is the one most commonly taught in

---

[2] See Leonard M. Kennedy, *Guiding Children to Mathematical Discovery* (Belmont, Calif.: Wadsworth Publishing Co., 1970), pp. 123-32, for a discussion of three methods.

the United States. Two reasons for
its popularity are that it clearly
shows subtraction to be the inverse
of addition and that each step with
the algorithm can be illustrated
with a place value device.

1. When decomposition is illustrated on a place value device,
only the minuend—67 in the
example at right—is shown. With
beansticks, begin with six tens
sticks and a 7 stick. Count two
beans on the 7 stick and note the
number left. Exchange the 7
stick for a 5 stick to show this
remainder. Remove three of the
tens sticks. The answer, or complete remainder, is represented
by the three tens sticks and the
5 stick.

Represent 67 on your abacus.
The subtraction is shown as two
beans are removed from the ones
rod and three are removed from
the tens rod. The answer is
represented by the beans that
remain.

2. Repeat the process with
beansticks and abacus as you and
your partner share explanations
for the following examples.

(a) 48   (b) 96   (c) 428   (d) 367
   −22   −35   −204   −246

3. The steps for subtraction
involving regrouping, or "borrow-
ing," are opposite those for
addition with regrouping. The
example at right illustrates this.
Represent the minuend, 62, with
beansticks. Note that there are
not enough beans on the 2 stick to
count seven; it is necessary to use
("borrow") one of the tens sticks
along with the 2 stick. Now count
seven beans and note the remainder.
Exchange the 10 and 2 sticks for a
5 stick. Remove three of the tens
sticks. The remainder, 25, is
represented by the two tens sticks
and the 5 stick.

67
−32

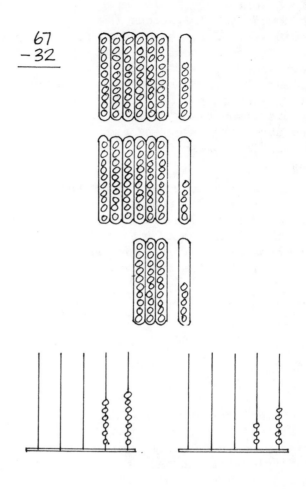

62
−37

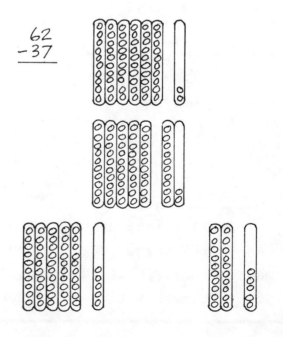

A series of similar steps is followed when the abacus is used. Begin with 62 represented on the tens and ones rods. To remove seven beans from the ones rod, take a bean from the tens rod and exchange it for ten on the ones rod. Now remove seven beans from the ones rod and three from the tens rod. The answer is represented by the remaining beans.

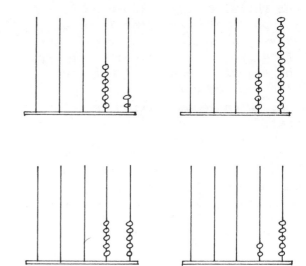

4. Explain to your partner the steps involved as you use beansticks and abacus to illustrate two of these examples. Listen to his explanation and observe his work with the devices as he illustrates the other two.

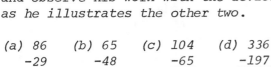

(a) 86   (b) 65   (c) 104   (d) 336
    −29   −48   −65   −197

ADDITION AND SUBTRACTION IN NONDECIMAL BASES

Children's work with addition and subtraction involving numbers expressed in nondecimal bases should be exploratory in nature. The activities are not intended to make children skillful in performing these operations with numbers expressed in bases other than ten, but they should help strengthen their skills with these operations expressed in their own system. As a result of their exploratory work, children should better understand the commutative (order), associative (grouping), and identity properties for addition and the algorithms for addition and subtraction.

---

1. Share these examples with a partner as you explain to each other how the abacus is used to illustrate addition and subtraction in nondecimal bases.

Base Five

(a) 23   (b) 21   (c) 104   (d) 421
    +21   +23   +132   +344

(e) 44   (f) 32   (g) 104   (h) 321
    −13   −14   −34   −134

Base Eight

(a) 32   (b) 41   (c) 324   (d) 362
    +41   +32   +156   +477

(e) 62   (f) 63   (g) 302   (h) 531
    −51   −45   −146   −157

2. Write the answer to each of the examples on your response sheet.

Magic triangles are introduced on the next MATHEMATICS CAN BE FUN page. Magic triangles are not as well known as magic squares, but they can also be used to help children see that mathematics can indeed be fun.

Mathematics Can Be Fun

MAGIC TRIANGLES

Here are two magic triangles.

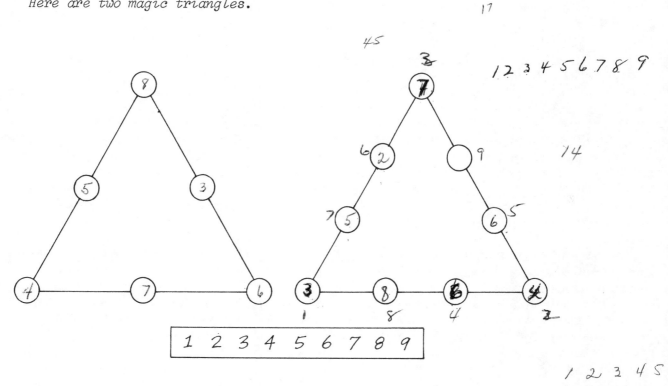

17

45

1 2 3 4 5 6 7 8 9

14

| 1 2 3 4 5 6 7 8 9 |

1 2 3 4 5
6

To complete the first triangle select *any six* of the nine numbers named in the box and arrange them in the rings so that the sum of the three numbers along each side is seventeen.

You use all nine numbers to complete the second triangle. Using each number only once, arrange them in the rings so that the *four* numbers along *each side* give the *same sum when added*. There are several ways to solve this puzzle, getting a different sum each time.

MULTIPLICATION AND DIVISION

Many children experience difficulty with the operations of multiplication and division. One reason is that <u>teachers</u> do not always <u>fully</u> comprehend these operations. Consequently children are often asked to <u>memorize</u> number facts that <u>lack meaning and to use</u> algorithms in a rote manner.

Three interpretations of multiplication are commonly used to help children grasp the meaning of the operation and its algorithms. One interpretation is that it is the mathematical operation that indicates what takes place when the union of two or more equivalent disjoint sets is formed. This "<u>repeated addition</u>" interpretation is most commonly used to introduce children to multiplication. Another interpretation is to consider it as the operation that indicates the number of objects in an array formed by some number of rows, each row containing the same number of objects. Finally, it is interpreted as being the operation that indicates the number of ordered pairs formed when each member of one set is matched with each member of a second, disjoint set. You will become acquainted with materials and procedures for helping children learn these interpretations as you complete the activities that follow. Remove the page of squares and strips, number lines, and Cartesian product charts from your manual. Cut out the squares and strips so you have one large square, ten strips, and one hundred small squares.

REPEATED ADDITION

1. Count a set of four small squares and put it on your table. Count another set of four squares and place it beside the first. Count a third set of four squares and place it beside the others.

The addition sentence that describes the situation when you join these sets is 4 + 4 + 4 = 12. The multiplication sentence is 3 × 4 = 12. Note that the first factor tells the number of equivalent sets, whereas the second factor tells each set's size. The product is the number of squares in the union of the sets.

2. Write the addition sentence, then the multiplication sentence, for each of the following situations.

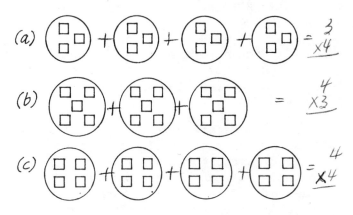

(a) = $\dfrac{3}{\times 4}$

(b) = $\dfrac{4}{\times 3}$

(c) = $\dfrac{4}{\times 4}$

3. Use your squares to illustrate half the following multiplication sentences for a classmate. Check his work as he illustrates the other half.

(a) 5 × 4 = $\dfrac{4}{\times 5}$ ☐   *(b)* 7 × 3 = ☐

(c) 6 × 3 = ☐   *(d)* 6 × 1 = ☐

(e) 3 × 7 = ☐   *(f)* 5 × 6 = ☐

4. The number line is effective for illustrating this interpretation of multiplication. The sentence 3 × 4 = 12 is illustrated on this line.

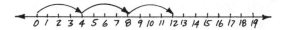

The first factor tells the number of jumps beginning at zero; the second tells the size of each jump. The product is named at the point where the jumps terminate.

5. Illustrate each of the sentences in Exercise 3 above on the first six lines on the number line page.

ARRAY

an array

6. *An array is an orderly arrangement of objects in which there are a
number of rows with the same number
of objects in each row. A "3 by 4"
array is one having three rows, each
containing four objects. (There
appears to be agreement among the
writers of mathematics programs
that the first factor indicates the
number of horizontal rows, and the
second indicates the number of objects in each row.)*

7. *With a partner use the small
squares to illustrate the arrays for
the sentences at the right.*

(a) $2 \times 3 = \square$ (b) $5 \times 6 = \square$

(c) $7 \times 1 = \square$ (d) $6 \times 5 = \square$

(e) $1 \times 7 = \square$ (f) $4 \times 4 = \square$

8. *Arrays are effective for illustrating the distributive property of
multiplication over addition. The
example at right begins with the display of a 2 by 12 array. As the two
sets of small squares on the right
are separated from the two tens
strips, 12 can be thought of as
10 + 2. Now there are two arrays—
2 by 10 and 2 by 2—and the steps
in the multiplication, either in the
sentence or algorithm form, are clear.*

$2 \times 12 = \square$

$2 \times (10+2) = \square$

$(2 \times 10) + (2 \times 2) = \square$
$20 \ + \ 4 \ = 24$

$$\begin{array}{r} 12 \\ \times\,2 \\ \hline 4 \\ 20 \\ \hline 24 \end{array}$$

9. *Select two of the following
examples and illustrate each with
strips and squares as you explain
the steps to a partner. He will
return the favor by explaining the
other two.*

(a) $3 \times 14 = \square$ (b) $6 \times 11 = \square$

(c) $5 \times 12 = \square$ (d) $4 \times 17 = \square$

10. *Multiplication involving pairs
of numbers greater than ten often
mystifies children. When children
work with squares, the mystery can
be swept aside.*
    *The example at right begins
with a 13 by 14 array. Separate
the four columns of strips and
squares on the right from the large
square and strips on the left;
think of the second factor as
(10 + 4). Rewrite the sentence
as 13 × (10 + 4) = $\square$, then as
(13 × 10) + (13 × 4) = $\square$. Next*

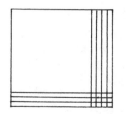

$13 \times 14 = \square$

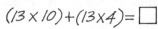

$13 \times (10+4) = \square$

$(13 \times 10) + (13 \times 4) = \square$

separate the three tens strips from the large square and the twelve small squares from the tens strips and rename the first factor as (10 + 3) and rewrite the sentences as shown beneath the illustrations. Again, the steps in multiplication with either sentences or algorithm form become clear.

11. *Illustrate and explain two of these examples for a partner, who again will return the favor.*

(a) *11 × 13 =* ☐   (b) *17 × 15 =* ☐

(c) *14 × 15 =* ☐   (d) *15 × 15 =* ☐

*12. Beansticks can be used in the same ways as the squares and strips. Use your set to illustrate some examples from Exercises 9 and 11 on pages 56 and 57.

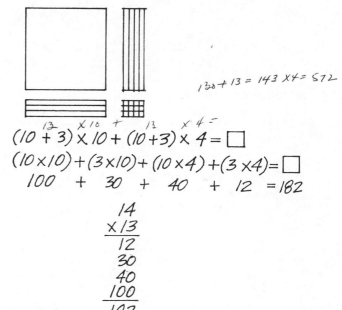

$130 + 13 = 143 \times 4 = 572$

$$(10 + 3) \times 10 + (10 + 3) \times 4 = \square$$
$$(10 \times 10) + (3 \times 10) + (10 \times 4) + (3 \times 4) = \square$$
$$100 \quad + \quad 30 \quad + \quad 40 \quad + \quad 12 \quad = 182$$

$$\begin{array}{r} 14 \\ \times\, 13 \\ \hline 12 \\ 30 \\ 40 \\ 100 \\ \hline 182 \end{array}$$

CARTESIAN PRODUCT

13. *Cartesian product charts provide a means for exploring work with this interpretation of multiplication. Fill in the left-hand column of the first chart with names of six different packaged cake mixes. For instance, the first you name might be "vanilla." Put the names of six different kinds of packaged frostings in the top row of the chart. Complete the chart by naming all the combinations of cakes and frosting*

you would get by using your frostings on your cakes. How many different cake-frosting combinations are there? If you have five cake mixes instead of six, how many possible combinations are there? If there are five of each, what number of combinations are there?

14. *Select another situation involving matching elements of two sets suitable for children and use it as you complete the other Cartesian product chart.*

The MATHEMATICS CAN BE FUN activity that follows introduces you to finger multiplication. Children are amazed to learn that they can multiply with their fingers, and they enjoy doing it once they learn how. It is a good activity for giving them a break in the routine of multiplying the usual way.

Mathematics Can Be Fun

FINGER MULTIPLICATION

Man's fingers have served as a "computer" for many hundreds of years. There is little doubt that our base ten numeration system had its beginning in man's use of his fingers for keeping track of numbers as he counted objects. There are few among us who have never counted on our fingers, but the use of fingers as an aid in multiplication is not well known, although it is possible to compute all products for pairs of numbers six through ten with them.

Hold both hands before you, thumbs up, so that you are looking at the palms. Number each finger on each hand, beginning with 6 for each little finger, 7 for each ring finger, and on to 10 for each thumb. Your finger computer is ready to use. Try it for the product of 7 times 8.

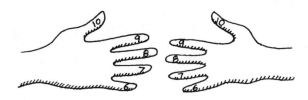

1. *Put the 7 finger of one hand against the 8 finger on the other.*

2. *Count the fingers on the left hand that are* **above** *the joined fingers. Then count the fingers on the right hand that are* **above** *the joined fingers. Multiply these two numbers. Your product is 6.*

3. *Count the two joined fingers and those* **below** *on both hands. There are 5.*

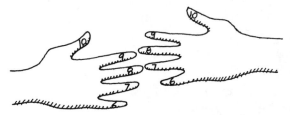

4. *The product of the two numbers for the "above" fingers on each hand is the number for the ones place of the product; the count of the "joined and below" fingers gives the number of tens. Thus we see that the finger computer gives the product 56 for the multiplication of 7 times 8.*

Try it for 8 times 8. What is the product of the two "above" numbers? What is the total of the "joined and below" fingers on both hands?

Demonstrate to a classmate how to use your finger computer for these multiplication sentences: 6 × 7 = 42, 9 × 9 = 81, and 8 × 9 = 72.

(Finger multiplication can be used for determining products for pairs of numbers greater than 10. See Louise R. Alger, "Finger Multiplication," The Arithmetic Teacher, *15, no. 4 [April 1968]: 341-43.)*

59

14   16
-7   -2
7   14
-7   -2
0   12

-2
12
-2
10
-2
8
-2
6
-2
4
-2
2
-2
0

(a) $14 \div 7 =$ (b) $15 \div 5 =$

(c) $16 \div 2 =$ (d) $20 \div 4 =$

(e) $13 \div 1 =$ (f) $21 \div 3 =$

Two different situations are commonly used to help children understand division. In both the problem begins with a set of known size. In one situation the problem is to determine how many members are in each of the several sets when the original set is separated into a known number of sets. In the other situation the problem is to determine how many subsets there are when subsets of known size are separated from the original set. The first type is a partitive situation; the second is a measurement situation. Use your small squares to acquaint yourself with these situations.

1. Count a set of fifteen squares. Now separate the set into three equivalent subsets. How many squares are in each subset? Did you put the squares into the subsets one at a time? Even though you may not have done this, you should recognize that this is a "one-for-Bob, one-for-Sue, one-for-me" type of situation. Children should be given frequent opportunities to visualize partitive situations by actually distributing objects in this fashion.

2. Count a set of twelve squares. How many subsets are there when you separate the set into subsets of three squares each? Note that the answer can be determined by a series of subtractions wherein 3 is subtracted each time. In measurement situations division is viewed as a form of repeated subtraction, and its relationship to the repeated addition interpretation of multiplication is emphasized.

12	9	6	3
-3	-3	-3	-3
9	6	3	0

3. Share these examples with a classmate as you each demonstrate to the other how squares are used to illustrate the two types of situations.

4. One way to help children understand division is to have them interpret story problems involving both partitive and measurement situations.

$\frac{16}{-4}$

(a) "Billy has sixteen cookies. He will share them equally among three friends and himself. How many cookies will each child get?"

(b) "Sally has twenty-one Storybook dolls. She plans to put them in boxes that hold three dolls each. How many boxes does she need?"

Although children need not be burdened with learning the names, they should learn to recognize whether a situation requires that they find the number of subsets (measurement) or the size of subsets (partitive). Identify the type of situation each of the above stories portrays. Make up one story problem of each type.

5. Measurement situations can be illustrated effectively on the number line. The sentence $12 \div 3 = 4$ is pictured on this line. The dividend, 12, indicates where the jumps begin, while the divisor, 3, indicates each jump's size. The quotient, 4, is the number of jumps.

Use the remaining number lines on the number line page to illustrate the first three examples in Exercise 3 above.

6. A repeated subtraction algorithm is commonly used to help children understand the steps involved when numbers greater than ten are used in division. How well a child understands this algorithm and later the conventional algorithm depends on how well he understands numbers and

the Hindu-Arabic numeration system and his ability to multiply by ten and multiples of ten and powers of ten and their multiples. There is evidence that a child's understanding is improved if he is familiar with measurement and partitive situations. The use of a story problem to set the stage for division encourages understanding. "We have 243 apples to put into boxes that hold 12 apples each. How many boxes do we need?" Now when the algorithm is discussed, the numbers represented in it have meaning: they tell how many apples are in the original set and the number that will go into each subset (box).

$$12\overline{)243}$$

As the division is considered, questions will guide children's thinking.

"Will we need at least 10 boxes?"

$$10 \times 12 = 120$$

"Will we need at least 20 boxes?"

$$20 \times 12 = 240$$

And so on. Record responses, as at right. This helps children see why 20 is a reasonable quotient and why 30 is not. Finally, use the algorithm to record the division. What is the meaning of the remainder 3 in this example?

"John has 375 stamps to mount for display. He will put them on 15 display cards. If he puts the same number on each card, how many stamps will each card have?" The algorithm is shown at right. What is the meaning of each number represented in it? The question-answer sequence might go like this: "What does '375' stand for?" (It is the number of stamps John has.) "Will John put at least ten stamps on each card?" (Yes.) "How do you know?" (10 × 15 = 150; he has more than 150 stamps.) "Will he put at least twenty stamps on each card?" (Yes. 20 × 15 = 300; he has more

than 300 stamps.) "Will he put at least 30 stamps on a card?" (No. He does not have enough stamps to do that.) "We know he will put at least twenty stamps on each card. How many more will he put on each one?" Children may respond by saying "4." If so, put "4 × 15" in the algorithm and subtract 60 from 75. The remainder, 15, indicates that there are enough stamps for one more on each card. This is recorded. Or the children may complete the work as in the algorithm at right, where they show that when 75 stamps remain there are enough for five more on each card.

7. Create a story problem similar to one of those given here. Then write a sequence of questions to guide children's thinking about the division. Use quotation marks around questions and parentheses around possible answers. Show the steps for completing the algorithm for your problem.

$$
\begin{array}{r|l}
12\overline{)243} & \\
\underline{240} & 20 \times 12 \\
3 &
\end{array}
$$

$$15\overline{)375}$$

$$
\begin{array}{r|l}
15\overline{)375} & \\
300 & 20 \times 15 \\
\hline
75 & \\
60 & 4 \times 15 \\
\hline
15 & \\
15 & 1 \times 15 \\
\hline
0 & 25
\end{array}
\qquad
\begin{array}{r|l}
15\overline{)375} & \\
300 & 20 \times 15 \\
\hline
75 & \\
75 & 5 \times 15 \\
\hline
0 & 25
\end{array}
$$

PLACE VALUE GROUPING BOXES

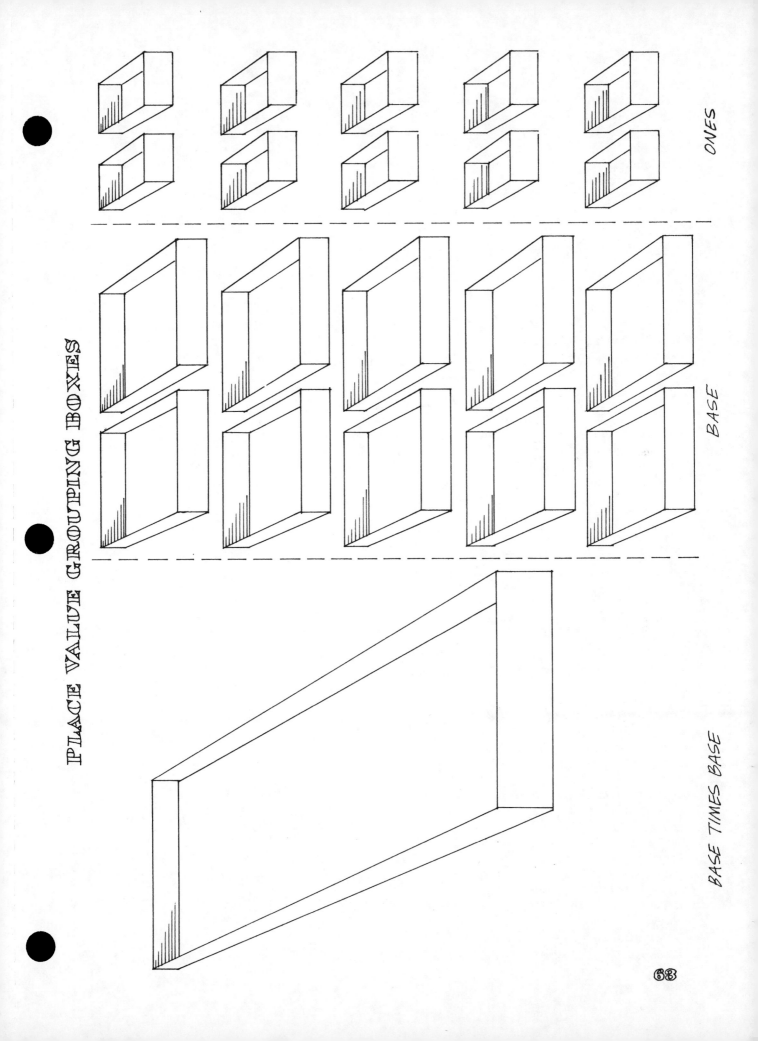

ONES

BASE

BASE TIMES BASE

63

ABACUS

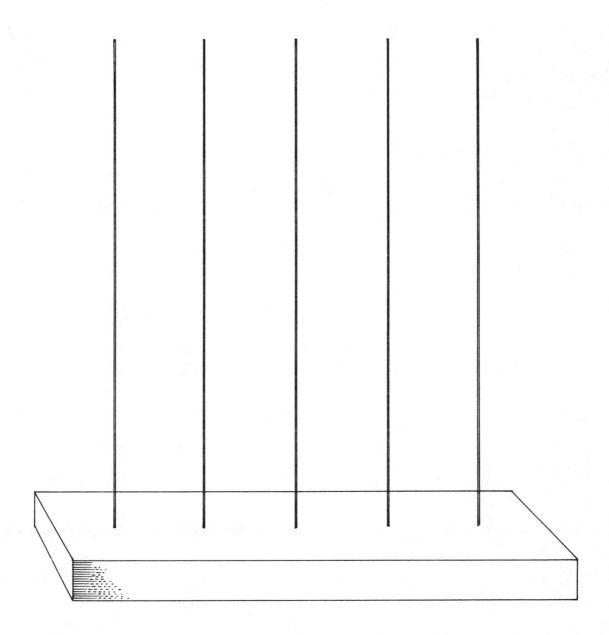

SQUARES AND STRIPS

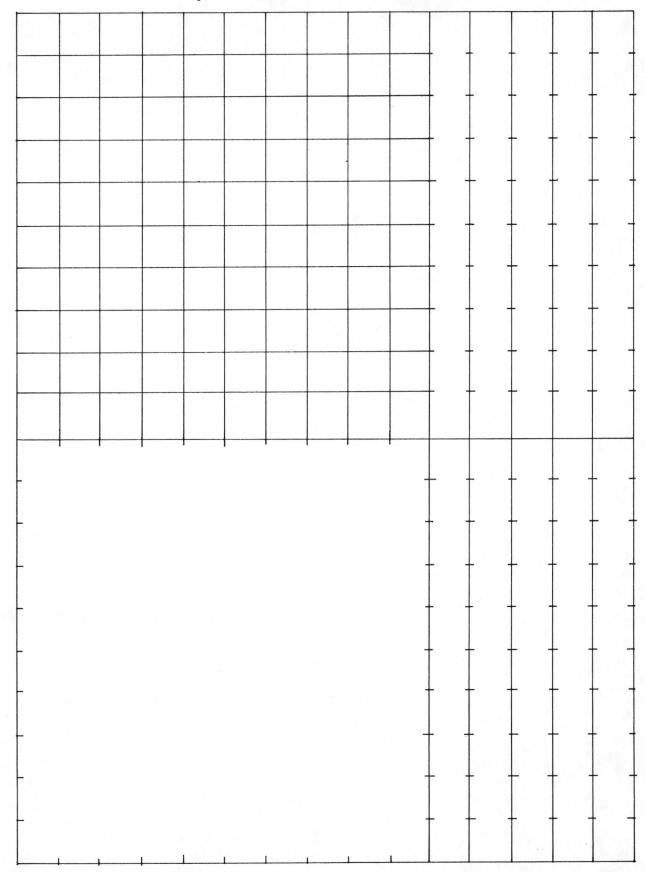

NUMBER LINES

a. 0 1 2 3 4 5 6 7 8 9 10 11 12 13 14 15 16 17 18 19 20 21 22 23 24 25 26 27 28 29 30 31 32 33 34 35 36 37 38 39

b. 0 1 2 3 4 5 6 7 8 9 10 11 12 13 14 15 16 17 18 19 20 21 22 23 24 25 26 27 28 29 30 31 32 33 34 35 36 37 38 39

c. 0 1 2 3 4 5 6 7 8 9 10 11 12 13 14 15 16 17 18 19 20 21 22 23 24 25 26 27 28 29 30 31 32 33 34 35 36 37 38 39

d. 0 1 2 3 4 5 6 7 8 9 10 11 12 13 14 15 16 17 18 19 20 21 22 23 24 25 26 27 28 29 30 31 32 33 34 35 36 37 38 39

e. 0 1 2 3 4 5 6 7 8 9 10 11 12 13 14 15 16 17 18 19 20 21 22 23 24 25 26 27 28 29 30 31 32 33 34 35 36 37 38 39

f. 0 1 2 3 4 5 6 7 8 9 10 11 12 13 14 15 16 17 18 19 20 21 22 23 24 25 26 27 28 29 30 31 32 33 34 35 36 37 38 39

g. 0 1 2 3 4 5 6 7 8 9 10 11 12 13 14 15 16 17 18 19 20 21 22 23 24 25 26 27 28 29 30 31 32 33 34 35 36 37 38 39

h. 0 1 2 3 4 5 6 7 8 9 10 11 12 13 14 15 16 17 18 19 20 21 22 23 24 25 26 27 28 29 30 31 32 33 34 35 36 37 38 39

i. 0 1 2 3 4 5 6 7 8 9 10 11 12 13 14 15 16 17 18 19 20 21 22 23 24 25 26 27 28 29 30 31 32 33 34 35 36 37 38 39

CARTESIAN PRODUCT CHARTS

FROSTINGS → CAKES ↓						
VANILLA						
Chocolate						
BANANA						
Choc. Chip						
Lemon						

RESPONSE SHEET

Whole Numbers

Name_____

Base Ten Numeration

Exercise 1 (pp. 40-41)

(a)   (b)

(c)   (d)

(e)   (f)

Exercise 2 (p. 41)

(a)   (b)

(c)   (d)

(e)   (f)

Exercise 3 (p. 41)

(a)   (b)

(c)   (d)

(e)   (f)

Exercise 4 (p. 41)

(c)   (d)

(e)   (f)

Exercise 5 (p. 41)

452,061 =

        =

        =

        =

Exercise 6 (p. 41)

Base Five Numeration

Exercise 2 (p. 42)   Exercise 3 (p. 42)   Exercise 4 (p. 42)

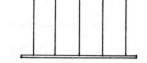

Base Eight Numeration

Exercise 6 (p. 42)   Exercise 7 (p. 42)

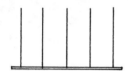

My numeral is:

Base Five Expanded Notation

Exercise 1 (p. 42)

Base Eight Expanded Notation

Exercise 2 (p. 42)

Characteristics Common to the Numeration Systems in this Workbook

Exercise 4 (p. 43)

Base Five Addition and Subtraction

Exercise 2 (p. 52)

(a)   (b)   (c)   (d)

(e)   (f   (g)   (h)

Base Eight Addition and Subtraction

Exercise 2 (p. 52)

(a)   (b)   (c)   (d)

(e)   (f)   (g)   (h)

Multiplication

Exercise 2 Repeated Addition (p. 55)

(a)   (b)   (c)

Division

Exercise 4 (p. 61)

(a)   (b)

Your two division story problems go here.   (Be certain you identify each
by telling which type it is.)

(a)

(b)

Exercise 7 (p. 62)

Your story problem, questions and responses, and algorithm go here.
(Attach another sheet of paper, if needed.)

4

Nonnegative Rational Numbers

Learning Centers

CHILDREN'S work with nonnegative rational (fractional) numbers deals with three ways of representing them: (1) common fractions, (2) decimal fractions, and (3) percent. Each experience a child has should bring him into contact with fractional numbers represented by physical models or used in familiar situations.

This chapter introduces the learning center approach to teaching mathematics by showing how children can learn about the common fraction form of representing nonnegative rational numbers in centers. Learning centers are one way to individualize instruction to meet children's varied needs and interests. A classroom may contain a single learning center dealing with one topic, such as addition of common fractions, or it may have several, each with its own topic. The centers will change as the topics under study change.

In some schools one room is set aside as a mathematics learning center. Here all mathematics equipment, supplies, and books are kept. One teacher is usually in charge of the center, working with children in small groups or complete classes. Often the center is organized into areas for computation, geometry, measurement, fractional numbers, games and puzzles, probability and statistics, and so on.

Activities in a center are usually directed by printed or recorded instructions or a programmed device of some sort. The teacher serves primarily as a resource person, assisting children as they select topics for study, answering their questions, furnishing equipment and supplies, and helping children evaluate their work.

The center approach can be adapted to many school situations. It can be used in a self-contained classroom, with team teaching in either graded or nongraded classes, and in departmentalized schools. It permits children to perform individual and small-group investigations yet allows the teacher to provide much or little supervision, depending on children's needs.

The learning centers in this chapter all deal with nonnegative rational numbers represented by common fractions.[1] The first center gives experiences for the eight- to ten-year-old child so that he can answer the question "What are fractional numbers?" At the second center, children compare fractional numbers. At center number three, the work deals with adding and subtracting fractional numbers. At center number four, multiplying and dividing fractional numbers are considered.

You will participate in the development of learning centers. You and several classmates may set up one of the centers described in this chapter, or you may design an original center with one or two of your classmates. Your instructor will help you organize to set up these centers.

At the conclusion of the experiences in this chapter you will be able to:

1. Use physical models to represent a fractional part of a unit or group.

2. Use physical models to illustrate the meanings of addition, subtraction, multiplication, and division of fractional numbers represented by common fractions.

3. Identify and use familiar situations to show applications of fractional numbers represented by common fractions.

4. Use the number line to order and compare fractional numbers.

5. Design and prepare materials for a learning center.

(The subject matter of the centers described here is presented in a sequence from simple to more complex, but the material in any one center or in the four centers does not provide comprehensive coverage of fractional numbers. The activities and materials are representative of types which might be included in learning centers dealing with these numbers.)

---

[1]The general plan of organization and format of materials for the centers in this chapter are based on the National Council of Teachers of Mathematics book, *Experiences in Mathematical Ideas*, Vol. I (Washington, D.C., 1970). Adaptation is made by permission of the Council.

LEARNING CENTER ONE: WHAT ARE FRACTIONAL NUMBERS?

The stations in this center provide materials for activities dealing with the meaning of fractional numbers represented by common fractions. Attention is focused on the relation of part to whole, where the whole is either a single unit or a set.

Performance Goal

The student who understands the concepts presented through activities at this center will be able to identify a fractional part of a unit or set, using both unit and nonunit fractions. (Note: A unit fraction has a numerator of 1; a nonunit fraction has a numerator greater than 1.)

Materials

The teacher's material packet, beginning on page 87, contains some of the materials to use in preparing each station of this and other centers. Student response cards, directions, and cards for envelopes can be removed from the manual and put on spirit duplicating masters by the copy machine process and printed in the quantities required for each station. You will need the following items for the stations at Learning Center One:

    8   3-5/8" x 6-1/2" white envelopes
    4   5" x 7-1/2" manila clasp
                envelopes
  Cuisenaire rods:
    14 white   2 yellow
     8 red   2 dark green
     3 green   1 black
     3 purple   2 brown
  Material from teacher's packet:
    Directions and cards for each
    envelope
    Response card for each student

Station I

This station will have four envelopes dealing with fractional parts of groups. Prepare each envelope by gluing its directions on the address side of a white envelope and putting its card inside.

Station II

Fractional parts of units represented by regions are the subject of this station. Directions and cards for the four envelopes are in the packet.

Station III

Cuisenaire rods are used in the envelopes for this station. Glue a brown rod in the space on the card containing the directions for envelope 1, then glue the card to the outside of a 5" x 7-1/2" manila envelope. Put one each of white, red, green, purple, yellow, and dark green rods inside the envelope. Envelope 2 will have a dark green rod glued in the space above the directions and will contain one each of white, green, purple, yellow, and black rods. Glue a brown rod on the direction card for envelope 3; put eight white and four red rods in the envelope. Glue a purple rod above the directions for envelope 4; put one green, two red, and four white rods inside.

Teaching Procedure

Class members will be organized into groups. The groups may involve all the class or only the portion who are working with fractional numbers at the moment. Each group is assigned to a station, at which children work singly or in pairs with material from one envelope. Each station has four activity envelopes, so prepare duplicates if more than four individuals or pairs are assigned to one station. Arrange for the exchange of envelopes and movement from one station to the next in an orderly manner.

LEARNING CENTER TWO: COMPARING FRACTIONAL NUMBERS

The number line can be used to order fractional numbers in sequence from smaller to larger. Once the numbers have been ordered on the line, it is possible to compare two or more numbers to determine which is smaller (less than), larger (greater than), or in between.

Performance Goal

The student who understands the number line chart will be able to use it to order fractional numbers in sequence and to compare one with another.

Materials

Make an enlarged copy of the number line chart from the teacher's material packet. A chart made on a large sheet of butcher paper with a scale of 32 inches between whole numbers is a good size. Use capital letters to identify the unnamed points on the chart. Use a copy machine to make a spirit duplicating master of the chart in the packet. Cover the heading at the chart's top so that only the line for the student's name and the chart are copied on the master. Make one copy for each student. Copy the problem cards on spirit masters and duplicate copies for the envelopes. For this center you will need:

1 number line chart (enlarged)
1 10" x 12" manila clasp envelope
2 6-1/2" x 9-1/2" manila clasp
           envelopes
Material from teacher's packet:
   Directions for each envelope
   Number line chart for Station I
   and problem cards for Stations
   II and III (prepare one for each
   student)

Station I

This station will have directions glued to a 10" x 12" manila envelope. Inside the envelope will be a copy of the number line chart for each student.

Stations II and III

Glue directions for each station to 6-1/2" x 9-1/2" manila envelope. Put enough problem cards inside each envelope so that each student will have one.

Teaching Procedure

Put the enlarged number line chart on the wall above this center's three stations. Organize the children into groups for each station, at which they will work singly.

LEARNING CENTER THREE: ADDING AND SUBTRACTING FRACTIONAL NUMBERS

Addition and subtraction of fractional numbers must be considered in relation to the types of situations that give rise to the operations. Examples of different situations that show some meanings of addition and subtraction are featured at the stations of this learning center.

Performance Goal

The student who understands the concepts presented through activities at this center will be able to add and subtract fractional numbers represented by fractions having common denominators.

Materials

The teacher's material packet contains directions for envelopes and problem cards for the stations at this center. Prepare duplicating masters of the response cards. You will need the following items:

4 6" x 9" manila clasp envelopes
Material from teacher's packet:
  Directions and cards for enve-
  lopes
  Response card for each student

Station I

This station will have two envelopes dealing with addition of fractional numbers. Prepare each one by
gluing directions to the outside of
a 6" x 9" manila envelope and putting
a problem card inside.

Station II

This station will have two envelopes dealing with subtraction. They
are prepared in the same way as those
for Station I.

Teaching Procedure

There are two stations within
this center, so organize the class
accordingly. It is suggested that
only a part of the class be assigned
to centers, while the remainder of
the children work at other tasks.

LEARNING CENTER FOUR: MULTIPLYING AND DIVIDING FRACTIONAL NUMBERS

It is easy to state rules for
multiplying and dividing fractional
numbers represented by common fractions. However, it is unlikely that
children will grasp the full meanings
of these operations unless they have
opportunities to use them in practical situations. Stations in this
center provide a means for investi-
gating practical applications of
multiplication and division of
fractional numbers.

Performance Goal

The student who understands the
concepts presented at this center will
be able to use physical models to
illustrate multiplication and division
sentences involving fractional numbers.

Materials

Remove the pages of materials for
this center from the teacher's material packet and complete the envelopes for each station. Some items
will need to be duplicated, so make
spirit masters of these. You will
need the following items for this
center:

20 lima beans
Paper strips 1" x 36" (one for each
student)
Ribbon 1/2" x 18" (use gift wrapping

ribbon, one piece for each student)
String 1-1/2 yards long (one piece
for each student)
8 6" x 9" manila clasp envelopes
Scissors (a pair for each student)
4 or 5 yardsticks
Material from teacher's packet:
  Directions, problem cards, and
  contents for each envelope
  Response card for each student

Station I

This station deals with multiplication. Three types of situations
are presented: in envelope 1, a
fractional number is multiplied by a
whole number (we may interpret this
as a repeated addition type of situation); in envelope 2, a whole number
is multiplied by a fractional number
(here we find a fractional part of a
group); and in envelope 3, a fractional number is multiplied by a
fractional number (here we find a
fractional part of a fractional part).
Directions, problem cards, and contents for envelopes are contained in
the packet, except for the lima beans
for envelope 2.

Station II

The student learns of situations
that call for division at this station. He sees that there are only

two such situations: partitive—"If I separate one-half of a unit into three pieces each the same size, what is the size of each piece?" and measurement—"How many halves are there in three units?" (Children need assistance to recognize that these situations are identical to those which call for division with whole numbers. Have children compare division with whole numbers to division with fractional numbers as you discuss the work they do at this station.) Envelope 1 will contain a 1" x 36" strip of paper for each student; envelope 3 will contain a half yard of ribbon for each student; and envelope 4 will have a one-

and-one-half yard piece of string for each one. Envelopes 2 and 5 contain material from the packet.

Teaching Procedure

There are places at the two stations for eight individuals or student pairs. Make duplicate copies of envelopes if more than this number of children will be at the center at one time. Students will be cutting and measuring, so allow ample room for them to work. Be sure there are places for them to deposit scraps and to put the materials they take from each envelope after they are finished with them.

LEARNING CENTERS FIVE, SIX, . . .

The subject and design of these centers will be selected by you and your classmates. One way to organize for working on their design and construction is on the basis of grade levels. Those who are interested in kindergarten or grade one can form one group, while those interested in other grades can form second grade, third grade, and other grade level groups. Another way to organize is by mathematical topic. For example, some of you may want to design materials for a center dealing with the decimal or percent form of representing fractional numbers. Others may want to organize on the basis of instructional materials. For example, you may wish to explore in greater depth possible uses of Cuisenaire rods.

Once a group is organized, you will need to select a subject for your center. You will find valuable help in subject selection from children's texts. Study copies of one or two of the mathematics series listed in Appendix A to see what topics are presented at each level. With this information in mind, you might choose to develop a center to use in conjunction with a textbook to reinforce children's understanding of concepts. Or, you might choose to adapt the material in the text to a learning center and use the center in place of the textbook. You should study books dealing with Cuisenaire rods and other special materials if you are interested in their uses in a center.

You will also find the series of booklets developed by England's Nuffield Mathematics Project (printed in this country by John Wiley & Sons) useful when you select a topic for your center and choose activities and materials to include in it. Two other books that will help are:

Biggs, Edith E., and MacLean, James R. *Freedom to Learn*. Don Mills, Ontario: Addison-Wesley Publishing Co. (Canada), 1969.

Kidd, Kenneth P.; Myers, Shirley S.; and Cilley, David M. *The Laboratory Approach to Mathematics*. Chicago: Science Research Associates, 1970.

Matchstick Puzzles are an old form of mathematical recreation. Three of these puzzles appear in the following MATHEMATICS CAN BE FUN activity.

Mathematics Can Be Fun

MATCHSTICK PUZZLES

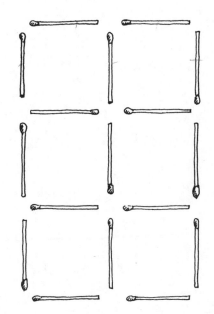

Seventeen matchsticks are arranged to form six squares. Five of the sticks can be removed to leave only half as many squares. Can you figure out which five you should remove?

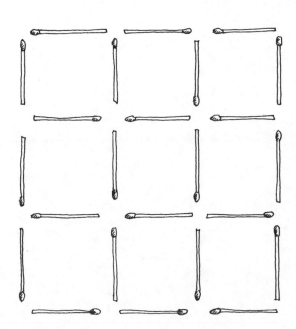

There are twenty-four matchsticks arranged to make nine squares. Remove four sticks so that there are five-ninths as many squares.

Begin with the same arrangement of twenty-four matchsticks. This time remove eight sticks to leave but two squares.

Envelope 1

1. One of the three circles is shaded. This circle is 1/3 of the set. Inside this envelope are four cards showing sets of circles. Select the card on which 1/4 of the circles is shaded. Write the card's letter on your response card.

Envelope 2

2. There are four cards in this envelope. On one of them 2/3 of the triangles are shaded. Write the letter of this card on your response card.

Cards 1

A

B

C

D

Envelope 3

3. Four triangles are pictured. Two are shaded. We can use both 1/2 and 2/4 to tell how many triangles are shaded.

Inside this envelope are four cards. One card shows 2/6 of the triangles shaded. Write its letter on your response card. Write another common fraction that tells the part of the triangles which are shaded.

Cards 2

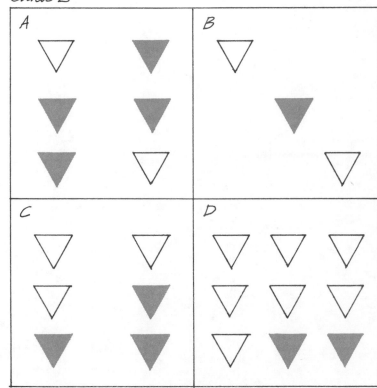

(Separate all cards along solid lines.)

87

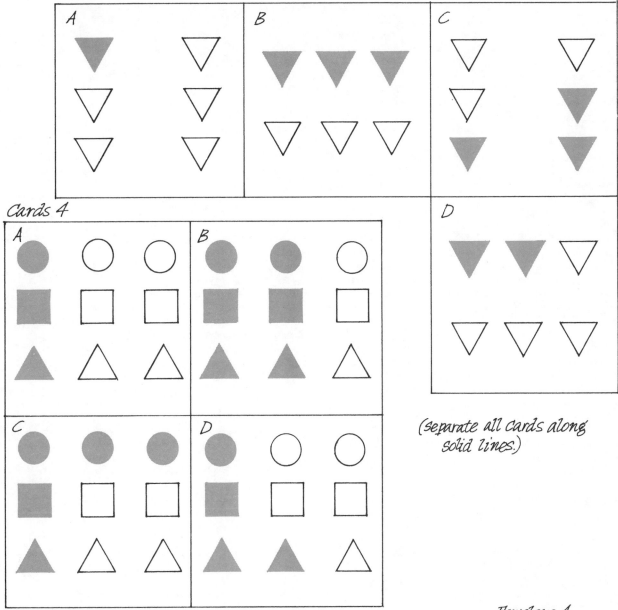

Cards 3

A

B

C

Cards 4

A

B

D

C

D

(separate all cards along solid lines.)

Envelope 4

4.

Inside this envelope are four cards. Each card has nine figures on it — three are circles, three are squares, three are triangles.

Write the letter of the card on which 1/3 of the figures are shaded.

Write the letter of the card on which 2/3 of the circles are shaded.

Envelope 1

1. 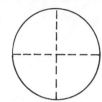 This circular region is cut into four parts that are the same size. Each part is 1/4 of the region.

Inside this envelope are four cards showing regions. Write the letter of the card on which 1/6 of the region is shaded.

Envelope 2

2. 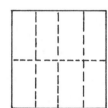 This square is cut into eight parts which are the same size.

There are four cards inside this envelope. On one of them 5/8 of the region is shaded. Write the letter of this card on your response card.

A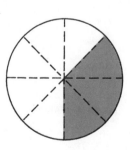

B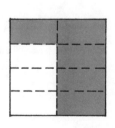

C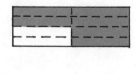

D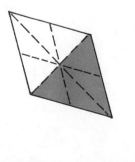

Cards 1

A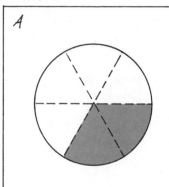

B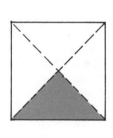

C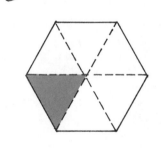

D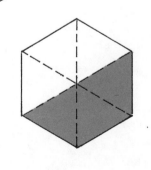

(separate all cards along solid lines.)

91

3.

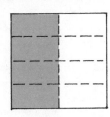

One-half of this region is shaded. Another name for 1/2 is 4/8.

There are four regions pictured on cards in this envelope. One shows that 3/4 and 6/8 are names for the same fractional number. Write the letter of this card on your response card.

4.

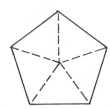

This pentagon is cut into five parts which are the same size. Each part is 1/5 of the region.

Inside this envelope are four cards showing pentagons. One shows that 2/5 and 4/10 name the same fractional number. Write the letter of this card on your response card.

Cards 3

A

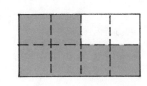

B

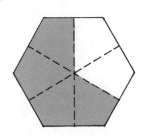

C

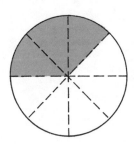

D

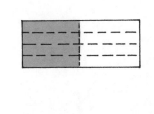

Cards 4

A

B

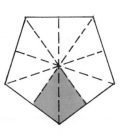

C

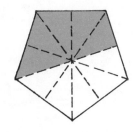

D

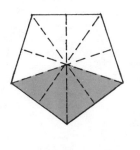

(separate all cards along solid lines.)

Learning Center One, Station III

Envelope 1

1.

Glue a brown rod here

Inside this envelope are six rods. One of them is ¼ as long as the brown rod. Write the color of this rod on your response card.

2.

Glue a dark green rod here

There are some rods in this envelope. One is ⅔ as long as the dark green rod. Write the color of this rod on your response card.

Envelope 2

Envelope 3

3.

Glue a brown rod here

There are some white and red rods in this envelope. Use them to complete these sentences:

a. One white rod is _____ as long as one brown rod.

b. Two white rods are _____ as long as one brown rod.

c. One red is as long as _____ white rods.

d. _____ and _____ name the same fractional number.

4.

Glue a purple rod here

Use the rods from this envelope to answer these questions:

a. When the purple rod is called 1 unit, what is the length of one white rod?

b. When the purple rod is called 1 unit, what is the length of one green rod?

c. When the purple rod is called ½ unit, what is the length of one white rod?

d. When the purple rod is called ½ unit, what is the length of one red rod?

Envelope 4

(separate all cards along solid lines.)

Number Line Chart

Number line 1: 2, 1, 0

Number line 2: 2, 4/2; 1, 2/2; 1/2; 0

Number line 3: 2, 8/4; 7/4; 6/4; 5/4; 1, 4/4; 3/4; 2/4; 1/4; 0

Number line 4: 2, 16/8; 14/8; 13/8; 12/8; 11/8; 10/8; 9/8; 1, 8/8; 7/8; 6/8; 5/8; 4/8; 3/8; 2/8; 0

Number line 5: 2, 32/16; 31/16; 30/16; 29/16; 28/16; 27/16; 26/16; 25/16; 24/16; 23/16; 22/16; 21/16; 20/16; 19/16; 18/16; 1, 16/16; 15/16; 14/16; 13/16; 12/16; 11/16; 10/16; 9/16; 8/16; 7/16; 6/16; 5/16; 4/16; 3/16; 2/16; 1/16; 0

Number line 6: 2, 6/3; 5/3; 4/3; 1; 0

Number line 7: 2, 12/6; 11/6; 10/6; 9/6; 8/6; 7/6; 1, 6/6; 4/6; 3/6; 2/6; 1/6; 0

STATION I

The number line chart shows common fraction names for some points that represent fractional numbers from 0 to 2. Some of the names for points on the lines have been left off.

Inside this envelope are copies of the chart. Take one and complete it by filling in the common fraction names for unnamed points.

STATION II

The number line chart shows that the point half way between 0 and 1 can be named 1/2, 2/4, 4/8, 8/16, and 3/6. (There are other names for this point.)

Inside this envelope are cards on which common fraction names for other points are given. Remove one of these cards. For each point that is named, list the other common fraction names given on the number line chart.

STATION III

The number line chart will help you compare fractional numbers. You can tell whether one number is larger or smaller than another or whether two numbers are equal. Also, the chart will help you put fractional numbers in order from small to large.

Take a card from this envelope and use the chart to help you complete it.

Learning Center Two
Station II   Name

a. 1/4

b. 16/16

c. 5/4

d. 6/8

e. 8/16

f. 30/16

Learning Center Two
Station III   Name

Put one of these signs in each number sentence to make it true: <, >, =.

a. 2/4   3/8   b. 7/10   2/3   c. 9/8   18/16

d. 3/8   5/16   e. 4/6   12/16   f. 29/16   11/6

Put these names for fractional numbers in order beginning with the name for the smallest number.

15/16, 7/8, 4/3, 1/2, 3/16, 1/8, 1/6, 18/16, 6/4.

(Separate all cards along solid lines)

Learning Center Three, Station I

Envelope 1

1.

When we add fractional numbers we may be using numbers that arise from measurement situations. The problems in this envelope deal with addition of measures.

Remove the problem card from this envelope. Write your answers on your response card.

Problem card

Station I   Problem card 1

When we measure things we often find that we must use fractional numbers to get a precise measurement. Look at these line segments:

Line segment AB is 2 7/16" long.

Line segment CD is 2 1/16" long.

Line segment EF is 2 9/16" long.

a. When we add the measures of segments AB and CD, we have the sentence 2 7/16 + 2 1/16 = ☐ . The sum is _____ .

b. Write the number sentence that shows addition of the measures for segments CD and EF. What is the sum?

c. Write the sentence for the addition of the measures for segments AB and EF. What is the sum?

d. Write the sentence for the addition of the measures of all three segments. What is the sum?

Envelope 2

2. When we add fractional numbers we may be joining subsets to form new subsets. The problems in this envelope deal with addition of subsets.

Remove the problem card from the envelope. Write your answers on your response card.

Problem card

Station I   Problem card 2

In these sets some of the figures are black, some are gray, some are white.

A ⬢⬢⬡⬡⬡   B ●●●●○○

C ▼▼▼▽   D ■■■■■

Write answers to these on your response card.
a. In set A, 1/5 is black, 1/5 is gray. 1/5 + 1/5 = ☐
b. In set A, 1/5 is black, 3/5 is white. 1/5 + 3/5 = ☐
c. In set B, 2/6 is black, 2/6 is gray. 2/6 + 2/6 = ☐

We can say that the black are 1/3 of set B. We can also say that the red and white are each 1/3 of set B. 1/3 + 1/3 + 1/3 = ☐

d. Use fractions to show the part of set C that is black; the part that is gray; the part that is white. Make up some sentences about set C. Be sure to include sums with your sentences.

e. Use fractions to tell the part of set D that is black; the part that is gray. Write a sentence about set D.

Learning Center Three, Station II

Envelope 1

1
When we subtract fractional numbers, we may be finding differences between the sizes of measures. The problems in this envelope deal with fractional numbers arising from measurement situations.

Remove the problem card from this envelope. Write your answers on your response card.

Problem card

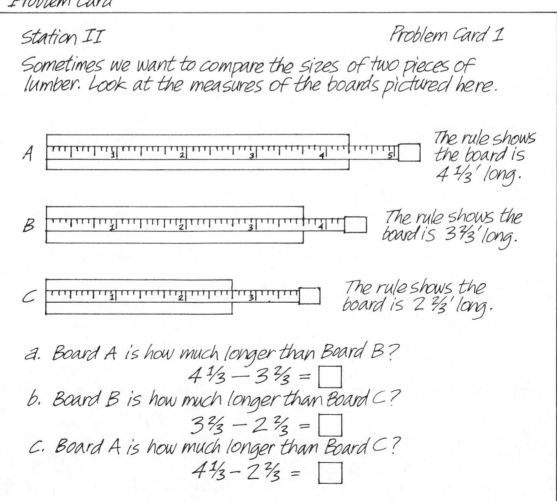

Station II   Problem Card 1

Sometimes we want to compare the sizes of two pieces of lumber. Look at the measures of the boards pictured here.

A   The rule shows the board is 4 ⅓' long.

B   The rule shows the board is 3 ⅔' long.

C   The rule shows the board is 2 ⅔' long.

a. Board A is how much longer than Board B?
   $4\frac{1}{3} - 3\frac{2}{3} = \square$
b. Board B is how much longer than Board C?
   $3\frac{2}{3} - 2\frac{2}{3} = \square$
c. Board A is how much longer than Board C?
   $4\frac{1}{3} - 2\frac{2}{3} = \square$

Envelope 2

2 We subtract fractional numbers when we compare parts of units. The problems in this envelope deal with comparisons of regions.

Remove the problem card from this envelope. Write your answers on your response card.

Problem card

Station II   Problem card 2

Pairs of regions are pictured here. Use them to complete the mathematical sentences.

A   B   C

a. How much more of the second circle is shaded than the first?

3/4 − 1/4 = ☐

b. How much more of the first square is shaded than the second?

2/3 − 1/3 = ☐

c. How much more of the second hexagon is shaded than the first?

3/6 − 1/6 = ☐

Envelope 1

1. Inside this envelope are strips of squares marked with letters, and a problem card. Remove one of the strips and the problem card. Cut out the squares, then cut each square into parts by cutting along the broken lines. Put all the "A" pieces in one pile, the "B" pieces in another, and the "C" pieces in a third pile.
Use the pieces to help you complete the problem card. Write your answers on your response card.

2. This envelope contains some lima beans and a problem card. Remove the beans and the card.
Use the beans as you complete the problem card. Write your answers on your response card.

Envelope 2

(separate all cards along solid lines.)

Problem cards

Station I

Problem Card 1

a. Put 4 of the "A" pieces together to form a square.
4 × ¼ = ☐

b. Remove 1 of the "A" pieces from your square.
3 × ¼ = ☐

c. When you use 6 "A" pieces, you can make a square and part of another.
6 × ¼ = ☐

d. Put 2 "A" pieces together, then put 2 more together, and finally, 2 more.
3 × ²⁄₄ = ☐

e. Put 2 "B" pieces together.
2 × ⅓ = ☐

f. With 4 "B" pieces you can make one square and part of another.
4 × ⅓ = ☐

g. Use "C" pieces to complete these sentences:
3 × ⅛ = ☐   5 × ⅛ = ☐   3 × ⅜ = ☐   4 × ⅛ = ☐

Station I

Problem Card 2

a. Count 15 beans and put them in 3 rows of 5 beans each.
⅓ × 15 = ☐☐
⅔ × 15 = ☐☐

b. Count 16 beans and put them in 4 rows of 4 beans each.
¼ × 16 = ☐
²⁄₄ × 16 = ☐☐
¾ × 16 = ☐☐☐

c. Count 18 beans and put them in 6 rows of 3 beans each.
⅙ × 18 = ☐
²⁄₆ × 18 = ☐☐
⁵⁄₆ × 18 = ☐☐☐☐☐
⁴⁄₆ × 18 = ☐☐☐☐

a. Count 15 beans and put them in 3 rows of 5 beans each.
⅓ of 15 =
⅔ of 15 =

b. Count 16 beans and put them in 4 rows of 4 beans each.
¼ of 16 =
²⁄₄ of 16 =
¾ of 16 =

c. Count 18 beans and put them in 6 rows of 3 beans each.
⅙ of 18 =
²⁄₆ of 18 =
⁵⁄₆ of 18 =
⁴⁄₆ of 18 =

3. This envelope contains small sheets of geometric regions and a problem card. Remove one sheet and the card. Cut out each region. Read the directions on the problem card before you cut the regions into pieces.

Write your answers on your response card.

(Cut here to separate)

Problem Card

Station I   Problem Card 3

a. Cut the square along the <u>broken line</u>. Each piece is $\frac{1}{2}$ of the entire square. Cut one of the halves into four pieces along the <u>dotted lines</u>. Each piece is what part of the square? $\frac{1}{4}$ of $\frac{1}{2} = \square$ $\frac{1}{4} \times \frac{1}{2} = \square$

b. Cut the circle into three pieces along the <u>broken lines</u>. Each piece is $\frac{1}{3}$ of the entire circle. Cut one of the the thirds into two pieces along the <u>dotted lines</u>. Each piece is what part of the circle? $\frac{1}{2}$ of $\frac{1}{3} = \square$ $\frac{1}{2} \times \frac{1}{3} = \square$

c. Cut the rectangle into four parts along the <u>broken lines</u>. Cut one of the fourths into three parts along the <u>dotted lines</u>. Two of these pieces are what part of the rectangle? $\frac{2}{3}$ of $\frac{1}{4} = \square$ $\frac{2}{3} \times \frac{1}{4} = \square$

(cut along this line to separate)

Sheet of regions for Envelope 3

Strips of Squares for Envelope 1

A   A

A   A

A   A

A   A

B

B

B

B

B

B

C   C   C   C

C   C   C   C

(cut along this line to separate)   111

Learning Center Four, Station II

Envelope 5

Envelope 1

1.

This envelope contains strips of paper. Each strip is 3 feet long. Take out one strip. Cut this strip into pieces so that each piece is 1/2 foot (six inches) long. How many 1/2 foot pieces did you get? Write your answer on your response card.

$$3 \div 1/2 = \square$$

2.

Inside this envelope are small sheets of paper on which are pictured four squares. Remove one sheet and cut out the squares.

Now, cut each square into fourths. How many of the fourth pieces did you get? Write your answer on your response card.

$$4 \div 1/4 = \square$$

3.

Inside this envelope are some ribbons. Each ribbon is 1/2 yard long. Take out one piece. Cut it into four pieces so that each piece is the same length. Each piece is as long as what part of a yard? Write your answer on your response card.

$$1/2 \div 4 = \square$$

Envelope 2

Envelope 3

5. Inside this envelope are papers showing a picture of 1/2 a cake. Remove one paper. If you cut 1/2 of a cake into pieces that are each the size of 1/6 of the cake, how many pieces will you get? Write your answer on your response card.

$$1/2 \div 1/6 = \square$$

4. This envelope contains pieces of string. Each piece is 1 1/2 yards long. Remove one of the strings. Cut it into three pieces so that each piece is the same length. Each piece is as long as what part of a yard? Write your answer on your response card.

$$1 1/2 \div 3 = \square \quad \text{or} \quad 3/2 \div 3 = \square$$

Envelope 4

Squares for Envelope 2 (do not separate)

Cake for Envelope 5

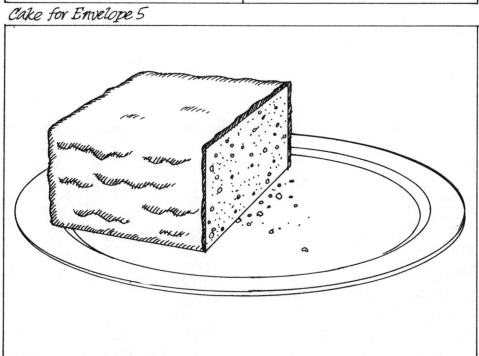

Response Cards for Learning Centers One and Three

RESPONSE CARD
LEARNING CENTER ONE

Name _____

STATION I

Envelope 1 _____
Envelope 2 _____
Envelope 3 _____ , _____
Envelope 4 _____ , _____

STATION II

Envelope 1 _____
Envelope 2 _____
Envelope 3 _____
Envelope 4 _____

STATION III

Envelope 1 _____
Envelope 2 _____
Envelope 3a _____ b _____ c _____ d _____ _____
Envelope 4a _____ b _____ c _____ d _____

RESPONSE CARD
LEARNING CENTER THREE

Name _____

STATION I

Problem Card 1

a _____
b _____ _____
c _____ _____
d _____ _____

Problem Card 2

a _____
b _____
c _____
d _____
_____
e _____

STATION II

Problem Card 1

a _____ b _____ c _____

Problem Card 2

a _____ b _____ c _____

Response Card for Learning Center Four

RESPONSE CARD
LEARNING CENTER FOUR   Name _____

STATION I

Problem Card 1   a _____ b _____ c _____ d _____ e _____ f _____

g _____ , _____ , _____ , _____

Problem Card 2   a _____ , _____ , _____ , _____ b _____ , _____ , _____ , _____ ,

_____ , _____ c _____ , _____ , _____ , _____ , _____ , _____ ,

_____ , _____

Problem Card 3   a _____ , _____ b _____ , _____ c _____ , _____

STATION II

Envelope 1 _____ Envelope 2 _____ Envelope 3 _____
Envelope 4 _____ Envelope 5 _____

5
Geometry

Problem Cards and Models

T HERE is probably no more striking example of the downward movement of mathematics from high school to elementary school than the inclusion of geometry in the mathematics program at all levels. Whereas formerly practically all geometry was confined to one grade of high school, today instruction begins in kindergarten and is included in each subsequent grade. Geometry provides a means for children to analyze the geometric properties of their physical environment. Activities with physical objects permit children to investigate and identify significant geometric concepts.

Problem cards are one means of guiding children's activities in mathematics. When they are used for geometry, single cards or a series of cards give directions for investigations dealing with geometric concepts. Children use geoboards and models of geometric figures while they work singly, in pairs, or in small groups. Because children can work independently, problem cards individualize instruction, yet by using multiple copies of cards a teacher can instruct an entire class at once.

The activities in this chapter will acquaint you with the geoboard and models of plane and solid figures. These devices provide the means for many classroom investigations. At the conclusion of these experiences you will be able to:

1. Use the geoboard to investigate concepts of plane geometry: line segments; closed figures, including polygons; points on, inside, and outside closed figures; and perimeter and area.

2.   Prepare problem cards for guiding children's investigations of geometric concepts.

3.   Identify characteristics of simple geometric solids (polyhedrons) included in the elementary program.

4.   Construct drawings of simple solid figures.

5.   Identify plane figures that have line symmetry.

6.   Identify the plane figures that are made when solid figures are sectioned in specific planes.

THE GEOBOARD

A geoboard[1] is a board on which pegs (nails) are arranged in some orderly fashion. Arrangements in common use consist of 9, 16, 25, and 36 pegs ordered in 3 by 3, 4 by 4, 5 by 5, and 6 by 6 patterns, with the 25-peg and 36-peg boards most popular. Boards having circular arrangements are also used.

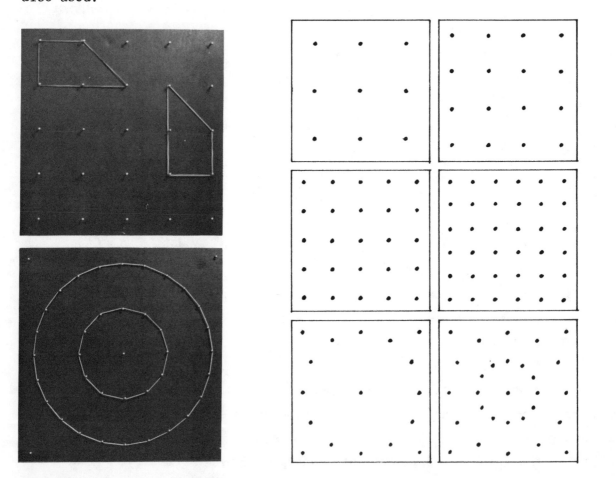

[1]Geoboards are manufactured by a number of companies, some of which are listed in Appendix B.

Colored rubber bands are stretched between and around pegs to provide visual images of geometric figures.

Geoboards can be used successfully at all grade levels for large and small group instruction as well as for individual investigations. Each child works with his own board and is encouraged to extend his investigations as deeply as his level of comprehension permits, so that even when they are working in groups, individuals are not restricted by their slower classmates. In general, children at all levels are introduced to geoboard activities by engaging in teacher-led investigations, although mature youngsters as low as grade two may begin by following suggestions provided on problem (task) cards. Later, problem cards can be used independently by most children, freeing the teacher to assist others in the class. The geoboard helps all children understand fundamental concepts of geometry. It also provides a means of investigation for children interested in pursuing topics to greater depth than other classmates.

The activities on the problem cards which follow have been chosen to introduce you to a variety of topics treated on a 25-peg board and a circular board. The cards should not be considered as a set that offers a sequence of activities for a particular topic, but rather as samples from selected areas of geometry. A response sheet, with dot paper, is included for your responses to investigations suggested on the cards.

1. LINE SEGMENTS — longer and shorter

Here are some line segments. Some segments are longer than others. Some segments are connected.

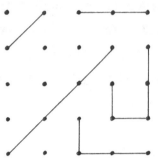 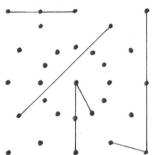

1. Form some line segments of your own. Make some long. Make some short. Show some on dot paper.

2. Form some connected line segments. Show some on dot paper.

2. CLOSED CURVES

Can you make these figures on your geoboard?

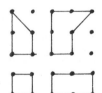 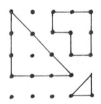 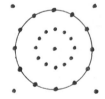

They are closed figures. Do you think you know why the word closed is used to describe these figures?

1. Make some closed figures of your own.

2. Make pictures of the figures you make on dot paper.

3. Can you name any of the figures on this card or on your dot paper?

3. POLYGONS

A <u>polygon</u> is a simple closed figure made from line segments. Some are pictured here:

Polygons have names associated with the number of sides and points they have. A <u>triangle</u> has 3 sides and 3 points. A <u>quadrilateral</u> has 4 sides and 4 points. An <u>octagon</u> is also pictured here. It has _____ sides and _____ points.

1. Make these figures on your geoboard:
   a. <u>Pentagon</u> — 5 sides and 5 points.
   b. <u>Hexagon</u> — 6 sides and 6 points.

2. Draw your pentagon and hexagon on dot paper.

3. Try to make a 2-sided closed figure. Do you see why the triangle is the polygon having the smallest number of sides?

4. QUADRILATERALS

Quadrilaterals have different shapes. Some are pictured and named here:

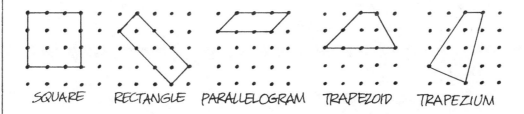

SQUARE   RECTANGLE   PARALLELOGRAM   TRAPEZOID   TRAPEZIUM

1. Make a different model of each figure on your geoboard.

2. Draw a picture of each of your figures on dot paper.

3. Study each figure carefully. Tell how you would describe each one to a friend.

5. INSIDE, ON, OUTSIDE

Reproduce each of the following designs on your geoboard:

(a) 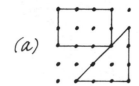   (b)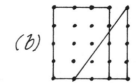

1. How many pegs are inside the triangle in (a)?
    (Remember that any peg touched by the rubber band
    is considered to be _on_ the figure.)
2. How many pegs are inside the triangle in (b)?
3. How many pegs are inside the rectangle in (a)?
4. How many pegs are inside the rectangle in (b)?
5. What is the number of pegs inside the rectangle, or
    triangle, _or_ both figures in (a)?

(over)

5. (continued)

6. What is the number of pegs inside both the rectangle _and_
    the triangle in (a)?

7. What is the number of pegs inside the rectangle, or
    triangle, _or_ both figures in (b)?

8. What is the number of pegs inside both the rectangle _and_
    triangle in (b)?

9. The sentences with "or" in them refer to (set union)
    (set intersection) situations.

10. The sentences with "and" in them refer to (set union)
    (set intersection) situations.

11. Make a design with two figures. Exchange yours for a
    classmate's and answer the same questions about
    his.

6. AREA

Four segments are joined to form a square. This square and all congruent with it will be described as having sides 1 unit long and an interior having an area of 1 unit.

1. Make a square that has sides twice as long. How many units of area are in the interior of this square?

2. Make a square having 9 units of area. How many units long is each side of this square?

3. What is the largest area you can enclose in a square on a geoboard with 25 pegs?

4. Which of these areas can you enclose in squares? Draw a picture of the ones you make on dot paper.

a. 1 sq. unit	d. 4 sq. units	g. 7 sq. units
b. 2 sq. units	e. 5 sq. units	h. 8 sq. units
c. 3 sq. units	f. 6 sq. units	i. 9 sq. units

7. AREA

1. Form a square having sides 2 units long. What is the area of the square's interior?
   a. Use another band to connect two opposite points to form a diagonal in the square. You now have 2 congruent triangles.
   b. What is the area of each triangle's interior?

2. Make a rectangle having one pair of opposite sides 3 units long and the other pair 4 units long.
   a. Use another band to make a diagonal in the rectangle.
   b. What is the area of each triangle's interior?

3. Do you see a relationship between the area of one triangle and the quadrilateral which contains it? Describe this relationship.

8. AREA

1. Make a rectangle with vertical sides 1 unit and horizontal sides 2 units long. What is the area of its interior?

2. Change the figure by moving the band around the top pegs 1 unit to the right. What is the area of the parallelogram's interior?

3. Make a 4 by 3 rectangle. What is the area of its interior?

4. Change the figure by moving the band around the top pegs 1 unit to the right. What is the area of the parallelogram's interior?

5. Can you use multiplication to find the area of a rectangle's interior? If you can, tell how you do it.

6. How can you use multiplication to find the area of a parallelogram's interior?

9. YOUR OWN PROBLEM CARDS

The area of a plane figure is the number of square units contained in its interior. The perimeter of a plane figure is the number of linear units contained in the line segments that form the figure.

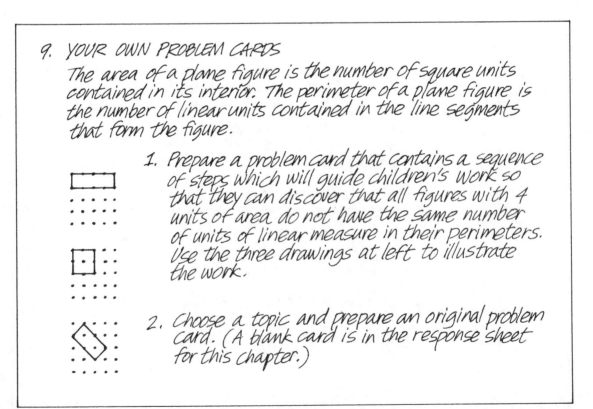

1. Prepare a problem card that contains a sequence of steps which will guide children's work so that they can discover that all figures with 4 units of area do not have the same number of units of linear measure in their perimeters. Use the three drawings at left to illustrate the work.

2. Choose a topic and prepare an original problem card. (A blank card is in the response sheet for this chapter.)

10 PROBLEM CARD REVIEW

Problem cards and/or manuals for geoboards are available from several publishers. You are encouraged to examine as many as possible. The materials listed here are recommended.

1. _Notes on Geoboard,_ Cuisenaire Company of America, Inc., (12 Church St., New Rochelle, N.Y. 10805),© 1967.

2. PROBLEMS: Green Set, Nuffield Mathematics Project, John Wiley & Sons, Inc. (New York),© 1969. (Not all activities on these cards deal with geometry.)

3. GEOCARDS: Geoboard Activity Cards.© 1970 by Houghton Mifflin Company,(Boston, Mass.).

4. _GEO SQUARE: Teacher's Manual_, by John Bradford and Harlan Bartram, Sigma Division, Scott Scientific, Inc. (P.O. Box 2121, Fort Collins, Colo. 80521),© 1967.

5. _Inquiry in Mathematics via the Geo-Board,_ by Donald Cohen, Walker (720 Fifth Ave., New York, N.Y. 10019),© 1967.

There are many puzzles based on geometric figures, especially on the square and cube. Tangrams and Madagascar Madness both have pieces cut from the square. Perhaps the most famous puzzle based on the cube is the Soma Cube, which is introduced on the next MATHEMATICS CAN BE FUN page.

Mathematics Can Be Fun

SOMA PIECES

There are seven pieces in a Soma set, each consisting of three or four cubes arranged in an irregular shape. No two pieces have the same shape. The seven pieces form all the irregular shapes that can be made using three or four cubes. You can make a set from 27 sugar or small wooden cubes and white glue.

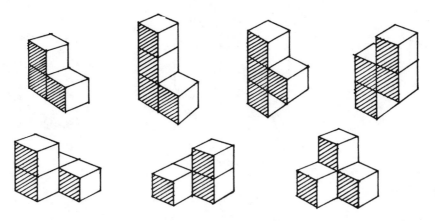

Many structures, including some rather fanciful ones, can be made using two or more pieces. Naturally structures made with all seven pieces are more complex than those constructed with a smaller number. You will find that working with the Soma pieces is both challenging and intriguing, as children do. As you work with them you will discover your sense of perspective growing sharper. Instead of employing a trial and error technique, analyze each pictured structure to visualize the way(s) it can be assembled. As a starter, put the seven pieces together to form one large cube. (It is claimed that there are more than 250,000 ways a cube can be formed, but you are not expected to find all of them; one will be enough.)

An element of competition is added when two or more players work with their pieces to see who can complete a given structure first. Children like to create and picture original structures. A collection of these can be assembled for a bulletin board or booklet as a class project.

Sample Structures

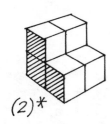
(2)*

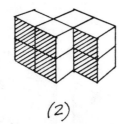
(2)

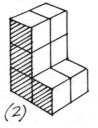
(2)

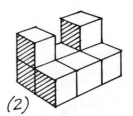
(2)

---

*The numerals in parentheses indicate the number of pieces required for the structure.

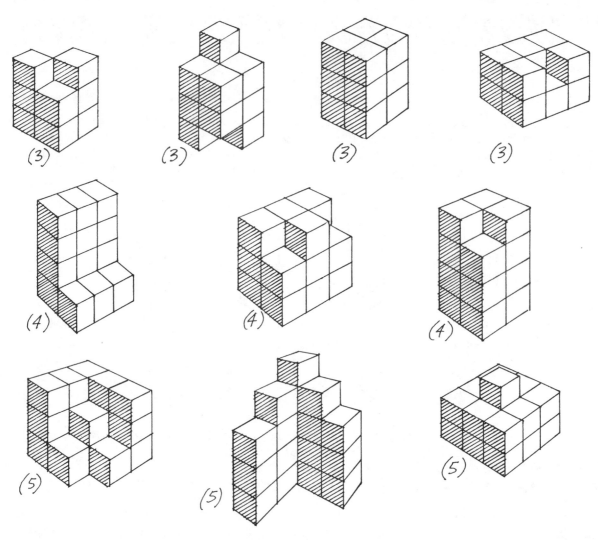

(3) (3) (3) (3)

(4) (4) (4)

(5) (5) (5)

These six structures require all seven pieces.

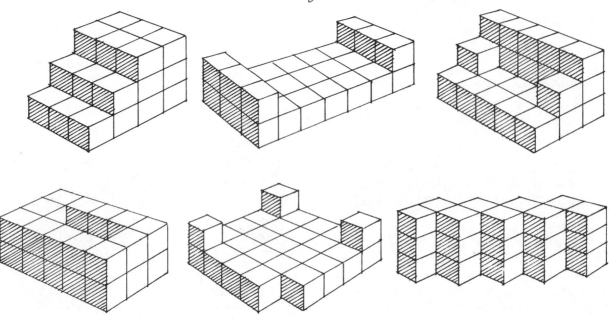

PLANE FIGURES

   *Models cut from paper or light-
weight tagboard to represent
regions formed by plane figures
serve as objects of study for many
pupil investigations. Children
can use them to investigate common characteristics such as sides,
vertices, and diagonals of polygons;
circumference, diameter, and radii
of circles; and types of triangles
and quadrilaterals.*

   *Investigations dealing with sym-
metry or plane figures can be made
with these paper models. Remove
the plane figure models on page
139 and cut them out. Use them
for the following activities.*

   *1. A plane figure is said to be
symmetrical, or have symmetry, if a
model of it can be folded in such a
way that the halves match exactly.
A figure may have one, two, three,
or more lines of symmetry. A square
has four lines, as illustrated at
right. Fold the figures cut from
your manual to determine the number
of lines of symmetry in each. List
your findings on your response sheet.*

   *2. Investigations into symmetry
yield opportunities for consideration of other characteristics of
plane figures. For example, while
you do the first investigation you
can also raise questions about the
relationship between the number of
lines of symmetry and the number of
sides in a regular polygon. (A
regular polygon is one in which all
sides are congruent.) What relationship do you see for the regular
polygons used in this investigation?
Write a statement about this relationship on your response sheet. Do you
believe this relationship holds true
for all regular polygons?*

   *3. For some of the polygons used
for the symmetry investigation, some
lines of symmetry are also diagonal
lines. What can you say about polygons for which this is true?*

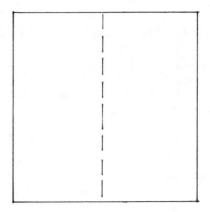

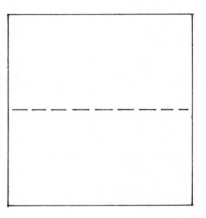

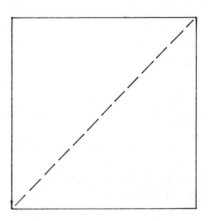

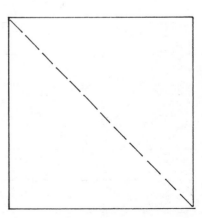

4. With scissors cut a piece of paper to produce a figure having only one line of symmetry, such as a conventionalized representation of a heart. A figure of this type has bilateral symmetry. Attach your figure to your response sheet.

5. Bilateral symmetry is common in nature. Make a collection of pictures of plants and animals that have bilateral symmetry. Attach your collection to your response sheet.

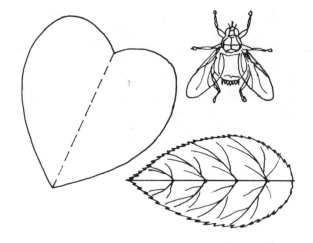

SOLID FIGURES

Children's work with solid figures is an essential part of their study of geometry. As children study models of three-dimensional shapes they extend their understanding of geometric concepts and learn to describe features of their physical environment. Cut out and assemble the models of solid figures from your manual. Also, get a small ball such as a golf, tennis, or styrofoam ball, and a cylinder, such as a small oatmeal box.

1. A polyhedron is a solid figure formed by the union of four or more polygons and their interiors. Among your polyhedron models are the five Platonic solids, which are distinguished from all others in that they are convex and each is formed by the union of four or more congruent regular polygons and their interiors. Name the five Platonic solids. Name the regular polygon associated with each.

2. Bring together your set of polyhedrons and after examining them, complete this table. Study the table to find a connection between the number of faces and

NAME OF SOLID	NUMBER OF FACES	NUMBER OF VERTICES	NUMBER OF EDGES

vertices and the number of edges in
each solid. Write a statement or
formula that expresses this relationship. The formula is referred to
as Euler's formula in honor of
Leonhard Euler, an eighteenth-
century mathematician who studied
this relationship.

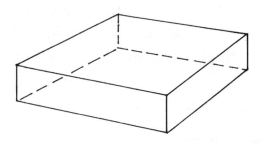

3. Children's study of solid
figures does not always involve the
use of three-dimensional models;
pictures of models are often substituted for the models themselves.
Before they can use a two-dimensional
picture of a three-dimensional object
meaningfully, however, children must
clearly visualize the model it rep-
resents. One way they can learn to
visualize pictures of solids is to
draw sketches of the simpler ones.
In geometry two types of pictures
are commonly used.

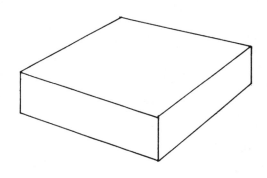

 a. Use one of your prisms as
 a model and draw a free-hand
 sketch of each type.
 b. Use one of your pyramids
 as a model and draw a sketch
 of each type.
 c. Use one of the solids
 associated with the circle as
 a model and draw a sketch of
 each type. (These solids are
 the sphere and cylinder.)

4. When a solid figure is sliced
straight through at some angle, a
plane section is formed. The face
of each plane section is in the form
of a polygon, circle, ellipse, or
other plane figure, depending on the
solid from which it is cut and the
way in which the slice is made.
Bring together your set of polyhedrons and figures associated with
the circle and examine each one carefully as you imagine the sections
that would be formed as different
cuts are made. Complete the chart
on your response sheet by listing
for each solid the names of several
of the plane figures made when it
is sectioned. (If you have diffi-

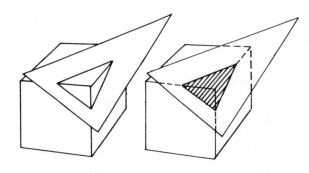

culty imagining the different plane
figures you can get, form some of
the solids with a piece of plastecine
clay. Then cut each of the clay
solids in as many different ways a
you can. Examine the face of each
cut to note its shape before you put
the figure back together for the
next cut.)

The Moebius strip, which is introduced in the next
MATHEMATICS CAN BE FUN activity, is a good "rainy-day"
activity. Each child in a class can make his own to
mark and cut. Suggest to the children that once they
have completed the activities given here they can make
more strips and cut them in other ways to see what
happens.

Mathematics Can Be Fun

MOEBIUS STRIP

The Moebius strip is certain to surprise those who are unfamiliar with it. Cut a strip of paper about 3 inches wide and 36 inches long. Make a band of it, giving it a half twist before gluing or taping the ends.

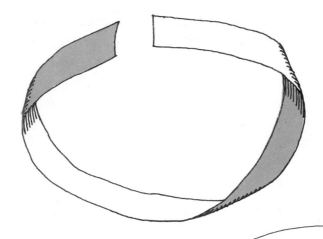

The first surprise comes when you mark a line on the strip with a crayon. Begin at any point on the inside of the strip and make a line midway between the edges by pulling the strip along the table beneath the crayon. What surprise do you find? Does the strip have an "inside" and an "outside"?

Now cut the strip along the line you marked. What is the surprise now?

Make another Moebius strip. This time cut it so the cut is about one-third of the way in from one edge. Are you surprised again?

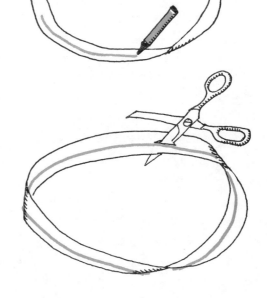

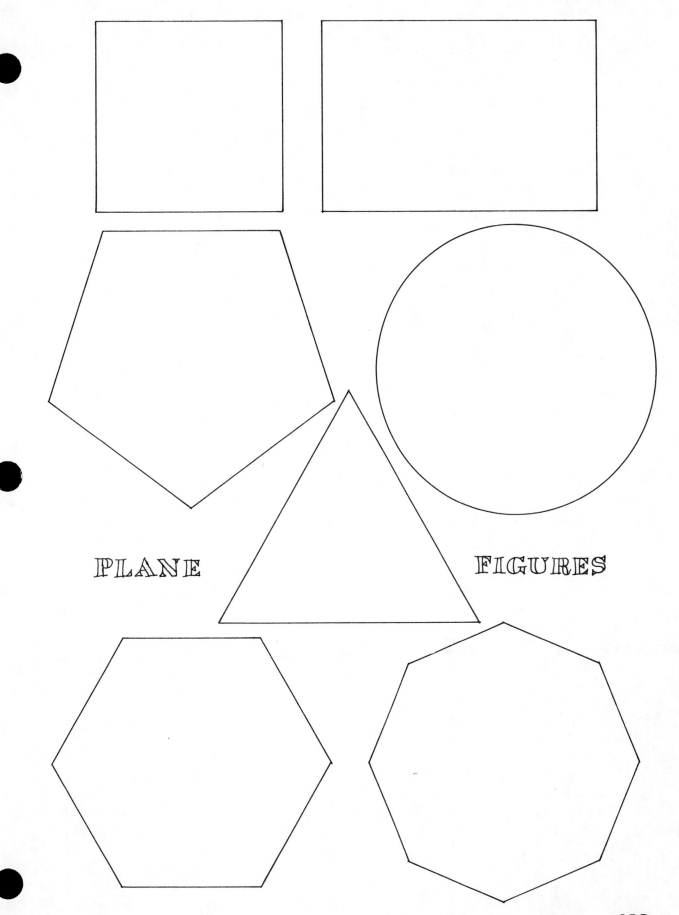

PLANE FIGURES

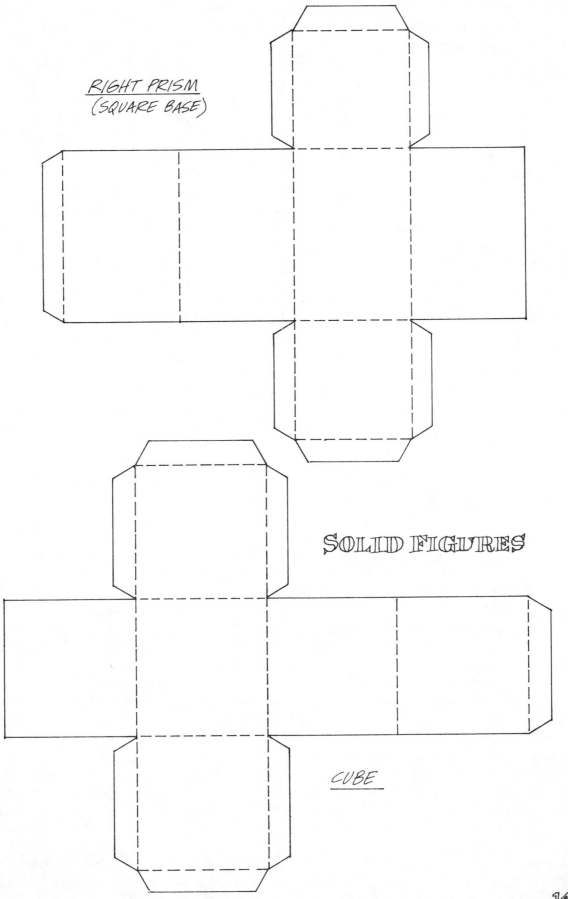

RIGHT PRISM
(SQUARE BASE)

SOLID FIGURES

CUBE

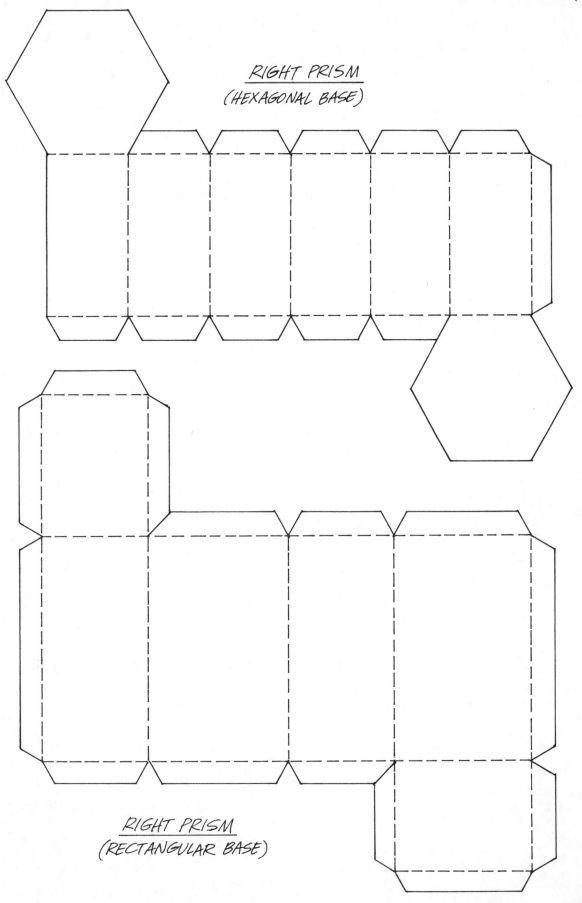

RIGHT PRISM
(HEXAGONAL BASE)

RIGHT PRISM
(RECTANGULAR BASE)

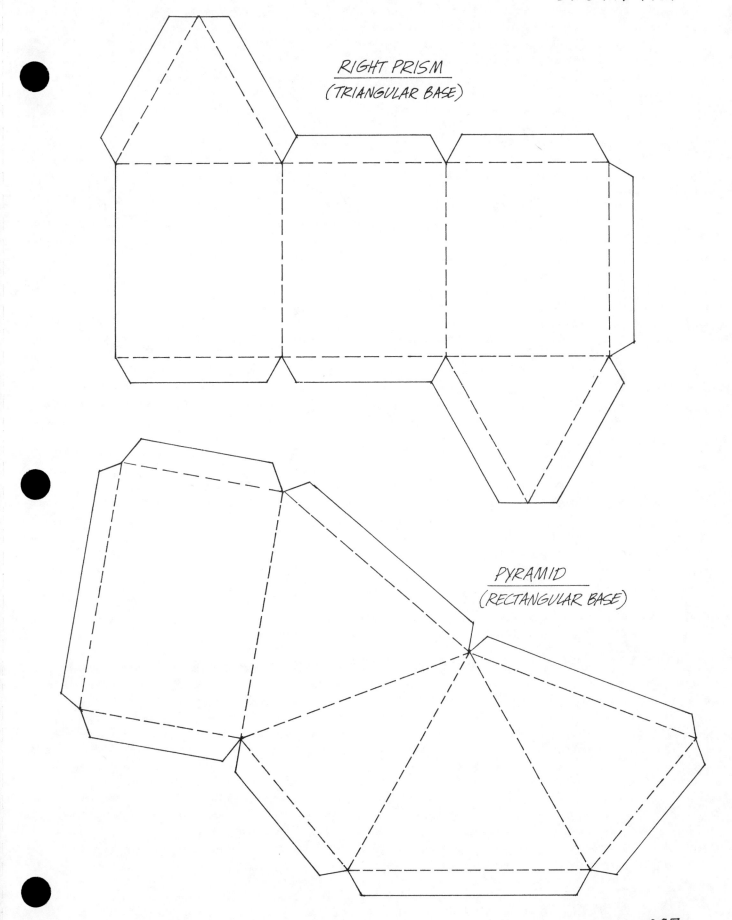

RIGHT PRISM
(TRIANGULAR BASE)

PYRAMID
(RECTANGULAR BASE)

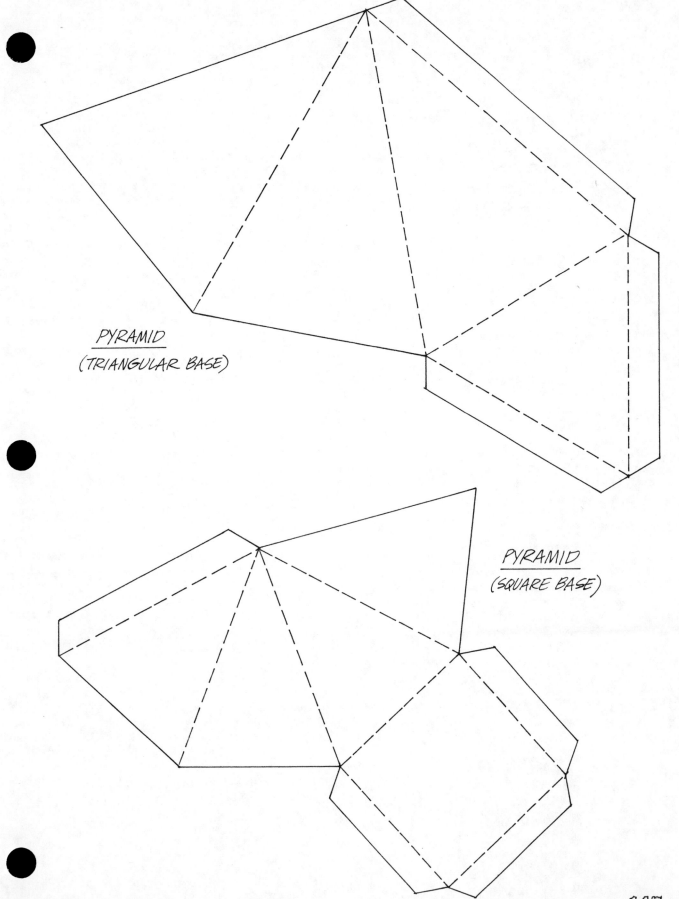

PYRAMID
(TRIANGULAR BASE)

PYRAMID
(SQUARE BASE)

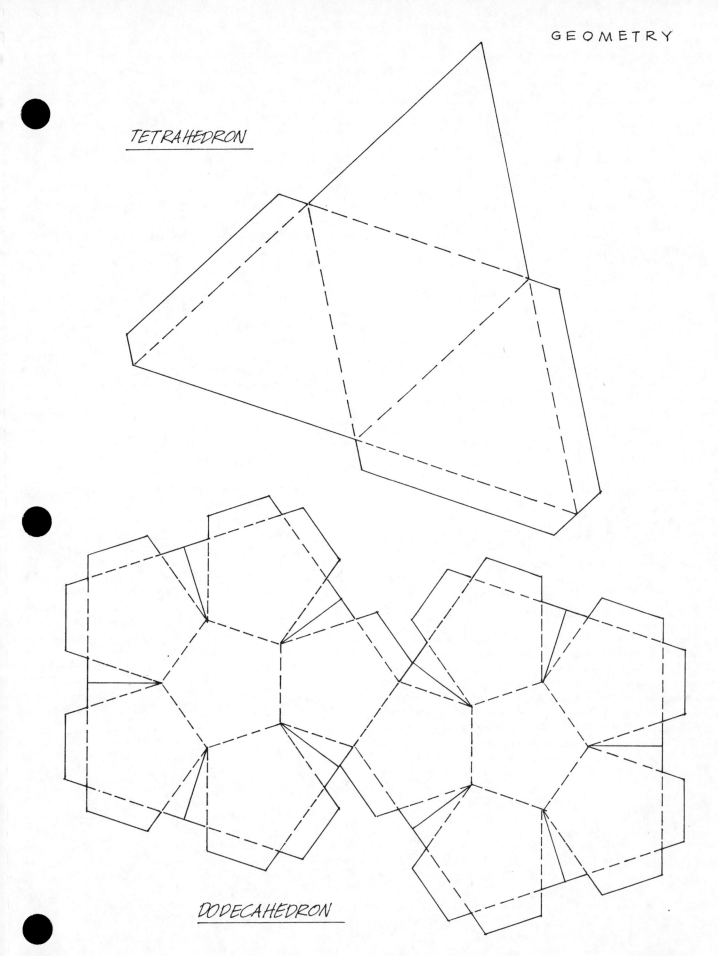

TETRAHEDRON

DODECAHEDRON

ICOSAHEDRON

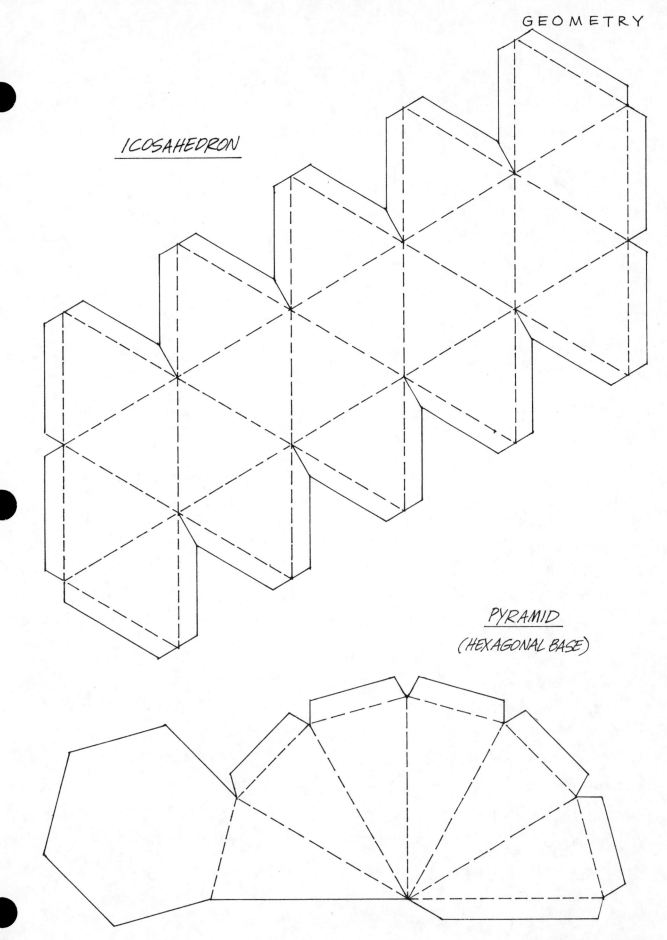

PYRAMID

(HEXAGONAL BASE)

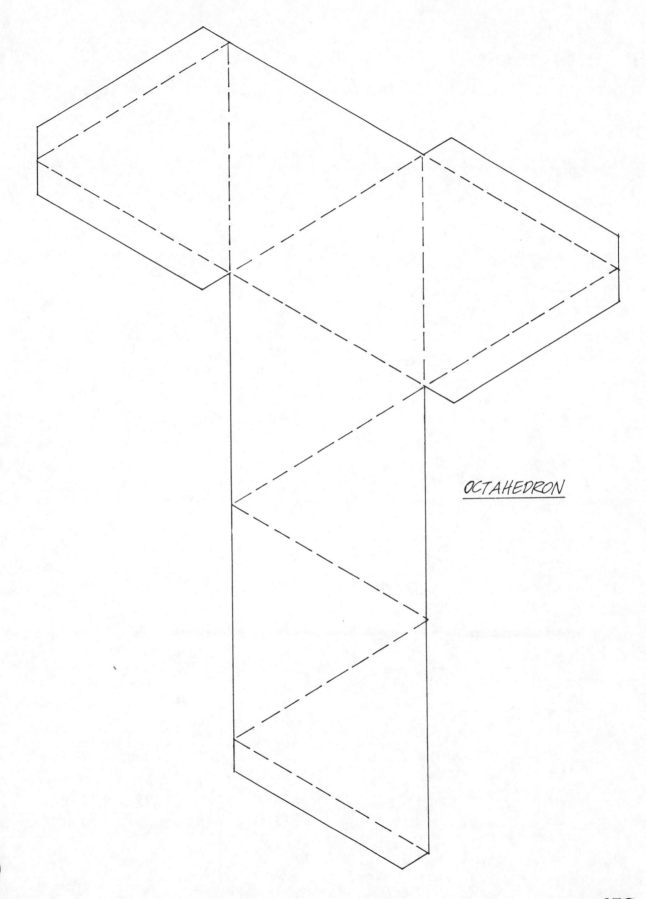

OCTAHEDRON

RESPONSE SHEET

Geometry

Geoboards   Name_____

4. Quadrilaterals (p. 125)

    3. _____

        _____

        _____

        _____

        _____

5. Inside, on, outside (p. 126)

    1. _____ 2. _____ 3. _____ 4. _____ 5. _____ 6. _____

    7. _____ 8. _____ 9. _____ 10. _____

6. Area (p. 127)

    1. _____ 2. _____ 3. _____

    I made squares having these areas: _____

7. Area (p. 127)

    1.b._____ 2.b. _____

    3. _____

        _____

        _____

        _____

Your Own Problem Cards (p.128)

9-1

9-2

8. Area (p. 128)

1._____ 2._____ 3._____ 4._____

5._____

_____

6._____

_____

Plane figures

1. Lines of symmetry (p. 133)

Equilateral triangle_____ Square_____ Circle_____

Rectangle_____ Pentagon_____ Hexagon_____ Octagon_____

2. _____

_____

_____

_____

3. _____

_____

_____

_____

Solid figures (pp. 134-135)

1. Five Platonic solids _____

_____

2. _____

_____

3. a.   Sketches of prism

    b.   Sketches of pyramid

    c.   Sketches of figure associated with circle

4.

Solid Figure	Plane Figures Made When Sectioned
a. Cube	
b. Right prism (square)	
c. Right prism (hexagon)	
d. Right prism (rectangle)	
e. Right prism (triangle)	
f. Pyramid (rectangle)	
g. Pyramid (square)	
h. Pyramid (triangle)	
i. Pyramid (hexagon)	
j. Tetrahedron	
k. Dodecahedron	
l. Icosahedron	
m. Octahedron	
n. Sphere	
o. Cylinder	

6
Measurement

Multimedia Devices

NOWHERE in their study of mathematics is it more important for children to engage in investigations leading to discoveries of concepts than during work with measurement. For too long in too many classrooms children's work has been confined to memorization of tables featuring information about linear, area, volume, liquid, time, and other measures. Children profit little from such activity. Some commit the facts to memory, but few gain much understanding of the systems studied or become competent users of instruments of measure.

At all levels of the elementary school, children must work frequently with measuring instruments—foot rules, meter sticks, scales for weighing, liquid containers, and so on. And although the English system is still the official system of measure in the United States, the need to work with the metric system and the instruments associated with it is increasing, because our country will soon be converting from the English to the metric system to bring us into conformity with the other major nations of the world. This change, which many persons believe is long overdue, will be hastened if advantages of the metric system over the English system are better understood by citizens. Such knowledge comes in part through activities dealing with the system.

Audiovisual learning aids such as reel and cassette tapes, records, overhead transparencies, filmstrips, films and film loops, and materials for multimedia devices can provide guidance for children's activities dealing with measurement. These materials and their playback and projector machines are easily handled and operated by most children, making it possible for individuals and small groups as well as an entire class to use the equipment.

At the conclusion of the experiences in this chapter you will be able to:

1. Write and record a script for a cassette and/or reel recorder to guide children's activities dealing with a mathematics topic.

2. Plan and prepare a sequence of frames for a filmstrip or a series of slides dealing with measurement.

3. Design and prepare a transparency with overlays to present information dealing with measurement.

4. Evaluate commercially prepared 16mm films, cartridge films, filmstrips, cassette and reel recordings, and overhead transparencies.

5. Describe the characteristics of multimedia devices and mathematics programs for them, such as Telor, AIM Tabletamer, Flex-Ed, Language Master, and Self-Instructional Basic Mathematics.

CASSETTE AND REEL RECORDINGS

In many schools cassette and/or reel recordings have become an indispensable part of the mathematics instructional materials. Recordings are used to guide children's investigations, to instruct them in new skills, and to give them practice with facts and algorithms. The cassette recorder/player is a particularly useful tool because of the ease with which recordings can be made and played on it. Children as young as kindergarten age can learn to use a cassette player independently. Both teacher-prepared and commercial tapes can be used by an individual child with a tape player that is equipped with a single earphone or by a group of children with a tape player that has multiple headsets without interfering with the activities of other children.

A number of companies have recorded programs of instruction on cassette or reel tapes or both. These programs generally include written materials to be used with the tapes. Use the tape evaluation report as you evaluate one or two of these programs. Listen to several tapes in each program and look over printed materials, if any, to form a clear idea of the mathematics covered and the mode of presentation. Appendix B provides a list of commercial tape programs.

Teacher-made tapes are generally of two types: those providing drill on the facts for an operation, such as addition, and those instructing children

TAPE EVALUATION REPORT

Name_____

Name of program_____

Authors_____

Company_____ Copyright date_____

This program consists of:

The mathematics topics included are:

It is designed for children who are:

Briefly, the procedure employed in this program is:

The program's strengths are:

The program's weaknesses are:

In general, my reaction to this program is _____

because:

in discovery or skill development activities. Simplest to make are those on which the basic facts for an operation are recorded. First record instructions about how to use the tape. Then dictate the facts in random order, using a rhythmic pattern with a regular time interval between each fact: "2 plus 3 equals . . .," pause, "6 plus 5 equals . . .," pause, and so on. After the last fact has been recorded, give instructions for checking the work, and finally, give the answers in the same order as the facts. The children's response sheet, which may be duplicated by either the spirit or the mimeograph process, will contain open sentences with room for written answers or lines for answers only, depending on whether children need both visual and auditory experiences while using the tape or only auditory experience.

Tapes designed for guiding children's work at a learning center or instructing a class in a new topic of study are more difficult to make. Keep your first efforts simple. Select a topic which can be presented without complicated instructions. Outline the sequence of steps to be included —that is, "set the plot." Write and edit your manuscript, then record it. Play the tape to check for technical details such as volume, tone, and voice quality, and for clearness of instructions. If there are any doubts about either technical details or clarity, correct the problems before giving the tape to children. If possible, observe children the first two or three times the tape is used to note their reactions. Note particularly the degree of interest they show and whether they have difficulty understanding. It may be necessary to revise a second or third time before your tape is effective. Once you become proficient in developing simple tapes you can expand your efforts to include scripts that have more complex plots and that require more than one voice or music or other sound effects. Some children may want to make recordings, too, and you should let them. It is a good way for them to demonstrate their understanding of mathematical concepts.

Scripts for two tapes follow. One is for use in primary grades to guide children's investigation into the relationships among half pints, pints, and quarts. The other introduces intermediate grade children to the origins of the metric system. Your instructor will assign to some of you the responsibility for recording one of these scripts and setting up learning centers in which they could be used. Each of you will also write an original script and describe a center for it.

TAPE RECORDING

Cartons That Hold Milk

If you have ever gone to the store to help buy groceries you have probably seen the cooler where milk is kept. Inside the cooler are cartons of milk, cream, and other dairy products. The work you do today will help you learn about the different cartons in which milk and cream are sold.

On the table are some milk cartons. There are small ones, middle-sized ones, and bigger ones. Count all of these cartons. (*Long pause.*) How many are there altogether? (*Short pause.*) Yes, there are ten of them.

Now, count the small cartons. (*Long pause.*) Did you count five of them? (*Short pause.*) The small ones are half-pint cartons.

Count the middle-sized cartons. (*Long pause.*) The three middle-sized ones are pint cartons.

There are two of the bigger cartons on the table. Pick up one of them. (*Short pause.*) Do you know what we call this one? (*Short pause.*) It is a quart carton. Find the words *one quart* on this carton. (*Short pause.*)

Milk is a liquid that can be poured from one carton to another and into a glass. You know that when milk is spilled it makes a mess. You are going to pour some milk, but it is going to be "pretend milk." Then if you spill some you can clean up your mess easily and quickly. You will use rice from the box on the table for your "pretend milk." You will also use the funnel when you pour the rice so you won't spill too much.

The first carton you will fill is one of the quart cartons. Do you remember that the biggest ones on the table are the quart cartons?

First put the small end of the funnel into the opening at the top of the carton. (*Long pause.*) Now fill the carton, using the can to take rice from the box. Turn off the recorder while you fill the quart carton. When the carton is full, turn the recorder back on. (*Short pause.*)

Now that you have filled the quart carton you will use the rice in it to fill the pint and half-pint cartons. Put the funnel into the opening of one of the middle-sized, or pint, cartons. (*Short pause.*) Pour rice from the quart carton until the pint carton is filled. Turn off the recorder while you do this. (*Short pause.*)

After you have filled one pint carton there is still rice in the quart carton. Put the funnel into another pint carton and fill it with the rest of the rice from the quart carton. Turn off the recorder while you do this. (*Short pause.*)

If you were careful and didn't spill too much rice and you didn't fill one pint carton too full, both pint cartons should have about the same amount of rice in them. Are both of yours filled almost to the top? (*Short pause.*) Two pint cartons hold as much milk as one quart carton.

You will now use the rice in one of the pint cartons to fill half-pint cartons. Put the funnel into one of the half-pint cartons. (*Short pause.*) Then fill it by pouring rice from one of the pint cartons. Turn off the recorder while you do this. (*Short pause.*)

Do you still have rice in your pint carton? (*Short pause.*) Use it to fill another half-pint carton. Turn off the recorder while you do this. (*Short pause.*)

You should have two half-pint cartons full of rice. Two half-pint cartons hold as much milk as one pint carton.

Pour the rice from the half-pint cartons and the other pint carton back into the box. Put the can and funnel in the box, too. Turn off the recorder while you do these things. (*Short pause*.)

See if you remember what you have learned about milk cartons during this lesson.

1. How many pint cartons did you fill with rice from one quart carton? (*Short pause*.) You filled two pint cartons with rice from one quart carton.

2. How many half-pint cartons did you fill with rice from one pint carton? (*Short pause*.) You filled two half-pint cartons with rice from one pint carton.

This is the end of this lesson. Rewind the tape and turn off the recorder.

NOTES

A long pause is ten to fifteen seconds; a short one is four to five seconds. Use your own judgment about the length of each pause, based on the reason for it. If you have or can get pictures of a grocery store dairy case, cows, dairy products, and other scenes related to processing and selling dairy products, use them for a bulletin board display near the work center where this tape is used. In many communities a branch of the National Dairy Council can supply all the pictures you need. Put a can in the box of rice. Have five half-pint, three pint, and two quart cartons at the center. Spread newspapers or newsprint on the table or floor—yes, the center can be on the floor—so that children can easily dispose of any spilled rice. Children should work singly or in pairs. Additional recordings should be made to direct children's investigations of the relationships between quart and half-pint cartons, quart and half-gallon cartons, and so on.

TAPE RECORDING

U.S. Is Inch Island in a Metric Sea

Not long ago an article entitled "U.S. Is Inch Island in a Metric Sea" appeared in a newspaper.[1] You may think that this is a strange heading for a newspaper article. What does it mean? What is an "inch island"? What is a "metric sea"? This heading and the answers to the questions won't make much sense to you until you know something about two measuring systems —the English system and the metric system—and where they are used in the world.

You are already acquainted with the English system, which is the official system of measurement for the United States. You know all about inches, feet, yards, rods, and miles; ounces, pounds, and tons; square inches, and square feet. Or do you? Let's find out. Take one of the work-sheets from the table and fill in the answers as you hear the sentences. Is your paper ready? (*Pause*.)

[1] *Sacramento Bee* (California), May 30, 1971, p. B5.

Here goes:

1. A quart has the same measure as ____ pints. (*Pause.*)

2. There are ____ inches in one foot. (*Pause.*)

3. A ton weighs the same as ____ pounds. (*Pause.*)

4. A yard measures the same as ____ feet. (*Pause.*)

5. ____ ounces weigh the same as one pound. (*Pause.*)

6. A gallon has the same measure as ____ pints. (*Pause.*)

7. There are ____ yards in a mile. (*Pause.*)

8. There are ____ square inches in a square foot. (*Pause.*)

Check your papers. Here are the answers:

1. A quart has the same measure as two pints. (*Pause.*)

2. There are twelve inches in one foot. (*Pause.*)

3. A ton weighs the same as two thousand pounds. (*Pause.*)

4. A yard measures the same as three feet. (*Pause.*)

5. Sixteen ounces weigh the same as one pound. (*Pause.*)

6. A gallon has the same measure as eight pints. (*Pause.*)

7. There are one thousand seven hundred and sixty yards in one mile. (*Pause.*)

8. There are one hundred and forty-four square inches in one square foot. (*Pause.*)

It wasn't too hard for you to fill in an answer for some of the sentences, was it? But did you fill all of them in correctly? Probably not. Very few people do. One of the reasons we find it hard to remember all the units of measure in the English system is that there are no consistent relationships between the various units. But this is not surprising when you consider how we got them.

Look at the chart of pictures showing the history of measurement. Look first at the one showing "The Inch."

It's the last picture in the top row. Read the caption to find out how we got the inch. Turn off the recorder while you do this. (*Pause.*) Who would have thought that the inch came from grains of barley corn? Look at the pictures about the yard and standard yard in the next row. Read the caption beneath each one. Turn off the recorder while you do this. (*Pause.*)

Use the yardstick to measure the distance between your nose and tip of the middle finger on your out-stretched arm. Be sure you use the yardstick and not the meter stick. You'll use the meter stick later. Turn off the recorder while you do this. (*Pause.*)

What did you find out? Is it thirty-six inches from your nose to fingertip? (*Pause.*) Is the measure of distance the same for you as your partner, or was it more for one of you than the other?

Look at the other pictures in the top and middle rows. Notice particularly what the captions say about the ways parts of man's body have been used for measuring. Turn off the recorder while you read the picture captions. (*Pause.*)

Do you see now why people are so often confused by the English system? The relationships among parts are not mathematical but are based on the human body, barleycorn, and other equally unrelated things.

Now let's look at the way the metric system was developed. You probably don't know very much about the metric system because it isn't widely used in our country. But it is used in all other major countries of the world, and one day it will replace the English system in our country.

Man made the metric system very differently from the way he made the English system. He invented the metric system in a very orderly fashion. Look at the globe and you will see how he did this. Find the string fastened to the globe. You should find one end at the North Pole and the other at a point on the Equator. Find the North Pole and the Equator. (*Pause.*) Now begin at the end on the Equator and trace the line toward the pole with a finger. Go slowly. When you cross the Mediterranean Sea and move into France slow down even more. Watch for the city of Paris. (*Pause.*) When you reach Paris, stop. (*Pause.*) Now finish tracing the path until you reach the North Pole.

Why trace a line through Paris from the Equator to the North Pole? Because that's how the metric system was invented. In Paris, France, in 1793, the French government announced that an entirely different system of measures was being adopted. This system was based on an imaginary line from a point on the Equator to the North Pole and passing through Paris. The scientists who invented the system cut this line into ten million parts, each of the same length. They called each of these ten million parts "one meter." Pick up the meter stick from the table. (*Pause.*) Compare it with the yardstick. (*Pause.*) Which is longer? (*Pause.*) Yes, the meter stick is a little longer.

Study the meter stick to see the way it is marked into smaller units of measure. What numerals do you see on it? (*5 to 10 second pause.*) Each numeral is at a point marked along one edge of the meter stick. Begin at "one" and count these marks from there to the other end of the stick. Turn off the recorder while you count the marks. (*Pause.*)

You should have counted 100 marks. If you only counted 99 you probably forgot that there is a mark at the end of the stick where "100" is.

The distance between each pair of marks is one one-hundredth of a meter long; this distance is called one centimeter.

Look at the meter stick on the bulletin board. Above it you see three lines. The word after each line tells how long it is. One line is a meter long, another is a decimeter long, and the shortest is a centimeter long. Study the meter stick and the information below it, and you should see why *centimeter* and *decimeter* are good choices for the units of measure they name. Turn off the recorder while you study the meter stick and other parts of the bulletin board. (*Pause.*)

The meter is the basic unit for measuring distance in the metric system. All other units of measure for length or distance in the system are based on the meter. The units for measuring area, volume, and weight are also based on the meter, as you will see when you study the system more during other lessons.

Now that you know a little bit about the metric system as well as the English system, let's think about that newspaper headline once again— "U.S. Is Inch Island in a Metric Sea." What does it mean? You will be able to understand its meaning when you have one more piece of information. Of the major nations of the world, only the United States has not officially adopted the metric system. We are the lone user of the English system among major nations. We are indeed an "Inch Island in a Metric Sea."

This is the end of this lesson. Rewind the tape and turn off the recorder.

NOTES

Pauses in this recording are of short duration except for those where times are given. The "History of Measurement" chart is available without charge from the Ford Motor Company, Educational Affairs Department (The

American Road, Dearborn, Michigan 48121). The string on the classroom
globe can be held in place with transparent tape. (When you remove the
tape pull it gently so that you do not damage the surface of the globe.)
Fasten a meter stick to a large piece of butcher or colored art paper.
Above the meter stick draw three lines—a centimeter, a decimeter, and a
meter long. Label these. Complete the bulletin board with information
that will help children see why *centimeter* and *decimeter* are appropriate
names for the units of measure they name. Put duplicated copies of the
quiz sentences near the recorder. Complete the center by furnishing a
yardstick and a meter stick. Assign children to the center in pairs.

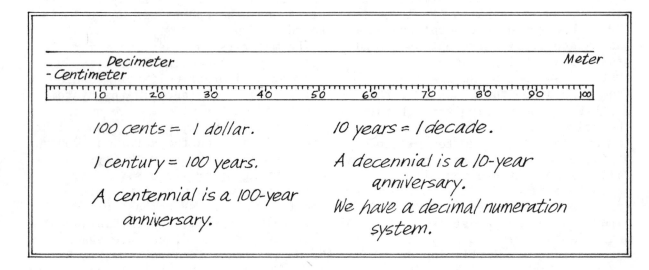

Following work at this center, children should move to other centers
where they measure objects using meter sticks and centimeter rulers. Additional tapes or problem cards or both can be prepared to direct these activities. Information about and suggestions for activities dealing with the
metric system and inexpensive meter sticks are available from the Metric
Association, Inc. (2004 Ash Street, Waukegan, Illinois 60085).

You will now prepare a script and recording. You may work alone or
as part of a small group. After you have recorded your script, set up the
center at which it will be used. Have several classmates listen to and
evaluate your tape and give suggestions for improving it and the center.
The following suggestions may help you choose a topic for your own tape
script.

1. Write a script for a subsequent lesson for one of the two given here.

2. Pretend that you are ill and write a script for a recording in which

a robot will replace you as teacher for a mathematics lesson. Choose your own topic.

3. Prepare a script which when used with a set of pictures or diagrams helps kindergarten and first-grade children recognize a simple geometric shape, such as a triangle or square.

4. Pretend that a man from outer space has prepared a tape explaining his numeration system, which has a base other than ten. Write the script. This is a good one to follow by having children prepare a tape explaining their own system, which in turn is sent to the man in outer space.

5. Imagine that an Egyptian, Roman, or some other person from ancient times recorded a message explaining his numeration system. The tape, along with some pictures, has just been "discovered" by an archaeologist. Write the script and draw the pictures for this message.

6. Imagine that Pythagoras is alive. You have attended a conference where you recorded a lecture in which he explains his theorem. Write the script for his lecture.

OVERHEAD TRANSPARENCIES

The overhead projector is one of the most widely used tools in mathematics classrooms. In many rooms it has replaced the chalkboard as a means of communicating ideas to help children understand concepts and processes. Its major advantages are:

1. It focuses children's attention on one idea at a time. The step-by-step development of an idea is provided for by the use of overlays, which may be added or subtracted to change the projected image.

2. The classroom is lighted in the normal manner, enabling students to use textbooks and other printed materials and to take notes while they view the projected material.

3. All transparencies required during the discussion of a given topic can be prepared in advance. These may be commercial or prepared by the teacher in color or black and white.

4. The teacher sits or stands facing the class, thereby maintaining eye contact with the students.

5. Transparencies can be used many times, and they are easy to store when they are not being used.

Commercial production of transparencies dealing with mathematics has expanded rapidly in recent years. Some publishers have produced sets to accompany their mathematics textbook series. The content of these projectuals reinforces that of the textbooks; a teacher's guide provides a key to their use. Sets not designed for use with particular textbooks are also available. A list of the names of some transparency sets and their producers is given in Appendix B. You should become acquainted with commercially produced transparencies. If you have the opportunity, develop a lesson using some and present it to a group of children. This will give you practice in using projectuals and will let you see how children react to them.

Teacher-made transparencies range from simple drawings made with a grease pencil on single sheets of clear acetate to those having color and several overlays for illustrating complex ideas and processes. Two transparencies, one dealing with the foot ruler and the other with area, are illustrated. Notes giving a brief explanation of each transparency and its overlays are written on the frames. These can serve as teaching cues while the transparencies are used.

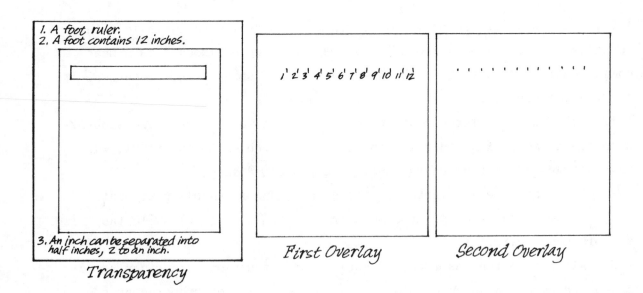

1. A foot ruler.
2. A foot contains 12 inches.

3. An inch can be separated into half inches, 2 to an inch.

Transparency

First Overlay

Second Overlay

Children who have been working with area measures will enjoy the next MATHEMATICS CAN BE FUN activity. The square can be duplicated by the spirit master process, or each child can make his own, using 1 inch squared graph paper.

Mathematics Can Be Fun

AN EXTRA SQUARE

A large square has 64 units of area if there are 8 square units along each side. Such a square is pictured here.

A curious thing happens when you cut out this square and then cut along the heavy lines to make four pieces. Reassemble the four pieces to make a rectangle, fitting them together as shown here.

Count the squares along each side of the rectangle. What is the product of 5 and 13? Can you account for the extra square?

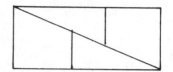

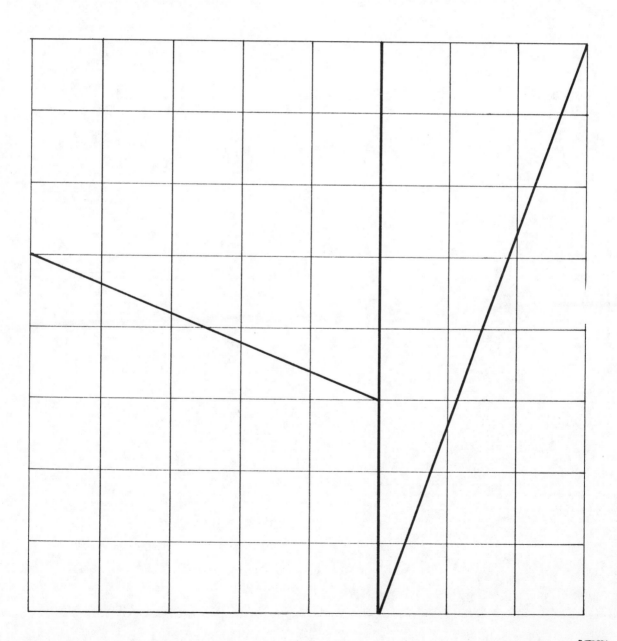

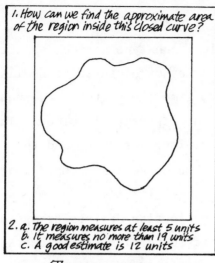

1. How can we find the approximate area of the region inside this closed curve?

2. a. The region measures at least 5 units
   b. It measures no more than 19 units
   c. A good estimate is 12 units

Transparency

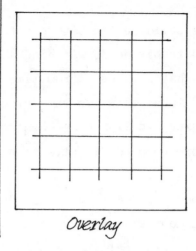

Overlay

Your first transparency should be kept simple, like the ones illustrated here. First select a topic dealing with measurement or some other area of mathematics. Then design the basic transparency and each of its overlays. Mark the transparency and each overlay with a sharpened grease pencil or fine-point, felt-nibbed pen, such as a Pentel Projector Marker. Finally, attach the transparency and overlay(s) to a cardboard frame. Use masking tape to fasten the transparency to the underside and as hinges to fasten each overlay to the top side of the frame. A masking tape tab should be attached to the free edge of each overlay to make it easy to turn.

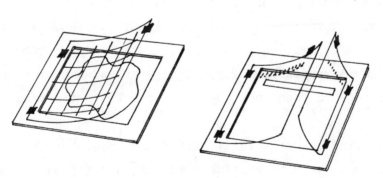

A second way to make transparencies is with sensitized acetate sheets, such as 3M Type 125 or 127.[2] Draw the pattern for each transparency and overlay on a separate sheet of white paper, using either a well-sharpened soft pencil or fine-point Speedball pen and India ink. Transfer the patterns to sensitized acetate by the copy machine process. Attach each piece to a frame in the manner already illustrated.

---

[2]3M Company, 3M Center, St. Paul, Minnesota 55101.

FILMSTRIPS AND SLIDES

Picture a child seated before a television-type screen, a pair of ear-phones fitted to his head, watching a series of pictures as he listens to a narration of what he sees. From time to time the picture and sound both stop and the child turns to write on a piece of paper at his elbow. The child resumes watching and listening when he finishes writing, and the picture and sound once more command his attention. The scene lasts approximately ten minutes.

Today's modern filmstrip and slide projection devices bring this scene to reality in many classrooms. Automatic sound filmstrip viewers, which project images onto small screens and use 33-1/3 records or reel or cassette tapes, combine visual and auditory effects to help children learn mathematical concepts and skills. Children can use these devices alone or in small groups and work independently of other classmates, or an entire class can view a filmstrip or set of slides. To do this, the teacher uses a machine which projects the film's images onto a large screen. Some large-screen projectors have synchronized record and/or tape or cassette players; others are without sound. The advantages of a pictorial representation are that pictures hold students' attention, clarify points by emphasizing the ideas being discussed, and provide a practical means of presenting information to individuals or small groups of children.

There are a growing number of mathematics filmstrips and slide programs designed for use with both small-screen and large-screen projectors. Some of these are listed in Appendix B. If you can, preview some of them, recording your reactions to each on a copy of the form that appears earlier in this chapter.

The teacher will find commercial filmstrips and slides useful. There are times, however, when none are available to fill a particular need. Then the teacher will want to prepare his own, using either a photographic proc-

---

The two puzzles on the next MATHEMATICS CAN BE FUN page have appeared in many guises. These and similar old puzzles have long intrigued puzzle fans.

Mathematics Can Be Fun

MEASURES AND WEIGHTS

An old-time marketplace is the setting for these two puzzles.

A dairyman opened his shop one day and discovered that some of the bottles he used to measure milk had fallen from the shelf and lay broken on the floor. Until he could get some new bottles he had only a 3-quart bottle and a 5-quart bottle to use. Yet when his first customer came in with a two-gallon container and asked for four quarts of milk the dairyman had no difficulty measuring out the correct amount. Can you tell how he did it?

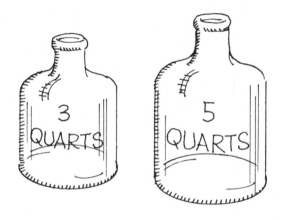

Next to the dairyman was a fruit dealer. The man used a balance scale and a set of weights to weigh fruit as he sold it. He had only five weights, yet he said he could sell fruit in bags containing any whole number of pounds up to 31 pounds. What weights did he have? Which would he use to weigh out 13 pounds of oranges?

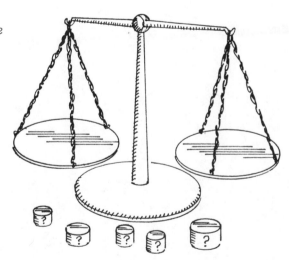

ess or pictures drawn on a special filmstrip material, called "U" Film.[3] A series of pictures processed as slides can also be used.

Making a filmstrip or a series of slides photographically requires more time and expense than drawing pictures on "U" Film. The photographic process should be used only when pictures will be used for a relatively long period of time. "U" Film can be reused, so it can be used for filmstrips having a temporary life as well as for those which will be used over a period of time.

The development of subject matter is essentially the same for both types of filmstrips and for slides. The only difference between the two filmstrips is that the content of each frame for "U" Film must be simpler than for photographed frames because of the limited space for drawings and captions. First write a performance objective for students who will use the film—"After viewing this filmstrip (set of slides) the student will . . . ." Then select content, both visual and verbal, to support this objective. As you select the content for each frame remember that the idea should be conveyed visually, with only limited verbal material to clarify the visual image.

A good way to organize your ideas is to use 4 inch by 6 inch cards, putting one idea to a card. Sketch the drawing for each frame in a square drawn on a card; put verbal content and notes alongside the sketch. Revise and rearrange the cards until they present the information in the best possible way. Make a final evaluation before producing your filmstrip or slides.

1. Does this slide help me achieve my presentation objective?

2. Is there good continuity between this slide and the previous one?

3. Does this slide *add* to my audience's knowledge of the subject?

4. Does this slide focus attention on one main idea? Is this idea clear?

5. Have I removed all unnecessary elements without destroying the one main thought in this slide?

6. Have I presented the information in this slide in the most effective manner?

---

[3]"U" Film is produced by Hudson Photographic Industries, Inc., 25 Buckhout St., Irvington-on-Hudson, New York, N.Y. 10533. The film comes in a kit containing film, a splicing device, containers and labels for finished filmstrips, colored pencils, and instructions.

7. Are the titles legible and short enough to be read in the time they will be shown?

8. Does the commentary add anything to this slide? Does it distract?[4]

When you use "U" Film you will draw the pictures and other visual material and write captions directly on the film, using either colored pencils from the kit or colored felt-nibbed pens, such as Dri Mark Communicators. When you use a photographic process, all pictures, charts, graphs, and other visual displays and captions must be prepared in advance and photographed. You must decide whether your presentation will be in filmstrip or slide form before photographing it. Pictures for a filmstrip must be photographed so that they are either side by side or one above the other and in sequence when the film is developed. After the material has been photographed, tell the processor whether to prepare the film as slides or a filmstrip.

While a tape narration is not necessary for all filmstrips, there are times when you want a tape so that the filmstrip or slides can be used by nonreaders or to heighten the manner of presentation. Music and other sound effects will often improve your production.

Topics dealing with measurement to consider for filmstrips or slides are:

1. Processes for measuring area
2. Concepts of liquid measure
3. Telling time
4. History of measurement
5. Measuring angles

Select one of these or a topic of your own choosing and prepare a set of cards with sketches, captions, and notes to illustrate your plans for its presentation by filmstrip or slides. If a narration will be part of your production, write the script for it.

---

[4]"Slides With a Purpose," Eastman Kodak Company, Rochester, New York 14650, p. 9. (Emphasis in original.) Used by permission. (This free booklet contains helpful suggestions for preparing slide film presentations, some of which have been adapted for this section. The suggestions apply to making filmstrips, also.)

FILMS

Educational films have been widely popular for several decades. Sound motion pictures, both black and white and color, are a vital part of the mathematics program in many classrooms. The ability of films to take children out of the classroom to far-off places or back in time to present historical events, to portray events by time-lapse photography and animation, and to stimulate children's imagination and understanding give them a unique instructional role.

The familiar 16mm film, which is projected onto a screen in a darkened room, has recently been joined by the 8mm loop, or cartridge, film, to give a teacher greater flexibility in using motion pictures. Educational 16mm films, with an average running time of eight to ten minutes, are usually presented for viewing by the whole class. Some of these films are used primarily to entertain and to stimulate children's interest in mathematics. One such film is *The Dot and the Line*,[5] a delightful tale of the romantic entanglement of a line (male) and a dot (female and a perfect 36-36-36). Other films are both entertaining and instructive. In the series of student films produced by the National Council of Teachers of Mathematics,[6] cartoon characters in films bearing titles such as *Between the Whole Numbers (Cavemen)* and *Shortcuts in Multiplying with Fractions (Mac's Factory)* lead children to discoveries of important mathematical concepts.

Eight millimeter cassette sound projectors and their cartridge-packaged films permit children to view films singly, in small groups, or as an entire class. A growing number of short, single-concept cartridge films are becoming available. See Appendix B for a list of some 16mm films and 8mm film loops and their producers.

The cost of projection equipment and films makes it mandatory that care be taken in their selection. The criteria for selecting projectors and screens will not be considered here. The film evaluation report form on page 189 will give you a means of recording your reactions to classroom films. The answers to these questions will help you determine whether or not you will use a film.

---

[5] Produced by Metro-Goldwyn-Mayer and distributed by Films, Incorporated, 1144 Wilmette, Wilmette, Illinois 60091.

[6] Distributed by Silver Burdett Company, Box 362, Morristown, New Jersey 07960.

Super 8 Projector-Screen, with
headphone attachment

Super 8 Film Cartridge

1.   Is the content worthwhile—that is, is it important that children
know what the film contains?

2.   Is the content mathematically correct?

3.   Does the film have good technical qualities—color, sound continuity,
acting, animation, and so on?

4.   Does the film present its content in a way children can understand?

5.   Can the content be presented in an equally effective yet less
expensive way?

6.   What does the film do that I cannot do in any other way?
The answers you give to questions 5 and 6 are of the greatest importance.
A positive answer to 5 and a negative answer to 6 will weigh heavily against
the use of a film, even though answers to the first four questions are all
in favor of the film.

PROGRAMMED DEVICES

Commercially prepared programmed devices are one means of individualizing
instruction.   These devices come in a variety of types at a wide range of
prices.   You can learn how these devices operate and about their programs

and functions by examining them, if they are available. Otherwise, you can begin by studying advertisements and pictures of some of the devices presently available. You can send for advertisements from these companies:

Tabletamer, Fractionfinder, and Matchmaker

  AIM Industries
  253 State Street
  St. Paul, Minn. 55107

Language Master (Arithmetic and Fraction Mastery Programs)

  Bell & Howell
  Audio Visual Products Division
  7100 McCormick Road
  Chicago, Ill. 60645

Flex-Ed (Program 305-M covers readiness and grades 1, 2, and 3)

  Educational Innovations, Inc.
  203 North 4th Street
  Carrollton, Ill. 62016

Self-Instructional Basic Mathematics

  Electronic Futures, Inc.
  57 Dodge Avenue
  North Haven, Conn. 06473

Telor Individual Instruction Tools

  Enrich
  3437 Alma Street
  Palo Alto, Ca. 94306

1. Consider the strengths of each device. Does it have observable weaknesses?

2. Can a teacher prepare his own programs?

3. Can the device be used to provide instruction over a fairly wide range of mathematical topics?

4. Can the basic equipment be used for instruction in other curriculum areas?

5. Which device(s) would you select if you were given the opportunity to choose?

FILM EVALUATION REPORT

Name of film _____

Producer _____

16mm_____ 8mm_____ Color _____ B & W _____ Running time _____

Brief description of contents _____

_____

_____

_____

Brief description of style of presentation _____

_____

_____

_____

I (will) (will not) use this film if it is purchased because

_____

_____

_____

_____

7

Probability, Statistics, and Logic

Games and Experiments

ACTIVITIES dealing with probability and statistics and with logic
introduce children to these topics in a general way. The main aim of
work in these areas is to help children to think clearly. In all fields of
mathematics, but especially in probability and logic, words have precise
meanings. It will not help children's thinking to have them memorize words
and their meanings, but there are many activities which help children to
develop an intuitive understanding of the language of mathematics and further their ability to think.

Games and probability experiments provide one means of introducing
children to probability, statistics, and logic. Games have been a part of
the instructional materials of mathematics for many years. Previously most
games gave the teacher a means of "sugar-coating" drill. Early games rarely
required children to think; rather, they provided opportunities to memorize
combinations and to practice basic skills. There is a continuing need for
games of this sort, and teachers should not overlook their value to the
mathematics program.

More recently, games and experiments which involve children in thought
processes more complex than memorization and recall have been developed.
The number of games dealing with probability and logic, as well as thought-
invoking games dealing with operations, sentences, and other topics and
books describing games, has increased markedly in the past decade. It is
possible to equip a mathematics laboratory with many commercial games and

much elaborate equipment. To the extent that a school has money to purchase these materials they should be made available to children. Care must be used in their selection, however, because there are many poor items.

None of the activities in this chapter requires elaborate or expensive equipment. Some of the materials can be purchased at a variety store toy counter; the rest are made by the teacher. In addition to the games and experiments presented here there are many others which deal with probability, statistics, and logic. Some of these you can make; others are commercially prepared. You should become familiar with as many of these as you can. Titles of books describing games and experiments and names of games and their manufacturers are given in the chapter to assist you. Games dealing with other aspects of mathematics and their distributors are listed in Appendix B.

At the conclusion of the experiences in this chapter you will be able to:

1. Describe at least four activities suitable for providing elementary school children with experiences dealing with probability and/or statistics.

2. Play at least four games for helping children gain an intuitive understanding of how words such as *and*, *or*, *all*, *some*, and *none* are used in mathematical logic.

3. Sort and classify elements in sets using both Venn diagrams and "tree" networks.

4. Describe at least three commercial activities dealing with probability, statistics, and logic.

ACTIVITY 1

CHICKEN RINGS

This is a simple activity in which plastic rings, commonly called "chicken rings," are used to introduce six- and seven-year-old children to simple ideas about probability and graphing. These rings can be purchased at toy counters and in fabric shops, where they are called stitch marker rings.

1. Select one or two classmates with whom to work.

2. Ask your instructor for a set of chicken rings.

3. Open the bag and put the rings on the table.

4. "Play" with the rings for awhile. What are some of the things you can do with them?

5. Put the rings back into the bag.

6. One player will draw a ring from the bag. Before the ring is drawn the drawer will predict its color. Was he right?

CHICKEN RING GRAPH

14				
13				
12				
11				
10				
9				
8				
7				
6				
5				
4				
3				
2				
1				

7. Replace the ring.

8. Repeat this activity several times. Keep a record of predictions, using a simple Yes and No tally system:

Yes ~~||||~~ No |||

Now remove the chicken ring graph page from your manual (page 193). Label each column with the name of one of the colors of rings. Place the graph on the table where all members of your group can see it. Draw the rings from the bag one at a time. Fill the chart, putting the first ring of each color in the box for that color opposite 1 at the bottom, the second opposite 2, and so on. Before each draw predict the color of the ring that will be drawn. Keep a record of predictions, as before.

With the completed graph before you discuss possible reasons for the results of your predictions. Why do you believe you had more right than wrong ones? (If you did, that is.) Why were your predictions wrong ones? (If that's the way they were.)

Before you leave this investigation, discuss some of the questions you might have children talk about while they work with chicken rings and the chart. Write your questions on paper and turn them in with the other papers for this chapter.

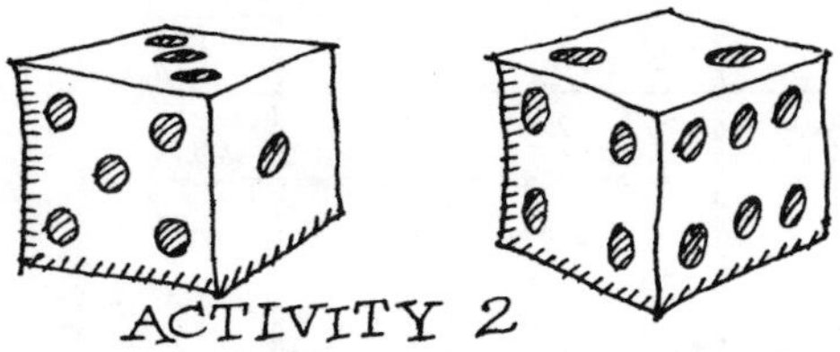

ACTIVITY 2

DICE

Dice are commonly used for probability experiments. They can be found in most toy stores and they cost little. You will need a pair of dice to investigate the frequency with which the sums 2 through 12 come up in a total of 50 rolls.

1. Get a pair of dice from your instructor. One die should be one color, the other a different color. Designate one die as the first die; the other will be the second die.

2. Remove the dice record sheet from your manual (page 197).

3. Roll the dice. Use a tally mark to record the result of this roll on your record sheet. For example, if the first die has 2 dots up and the second has 4, the tally will go in the row next to the 2 and under the 4.

4. Do this for a total of 50 rolls.

5. Fill in the blanks at the bottom of the record sheet.

6. Sign the form and turn it in to your instructor or the student who is serving as collector.

If you have the opportunity, challenge a class of fourth-, fifth-, or sixth-graders with this: "I will roll these dice and give you a point if the total is 2, 3, 4, 10, 11, or 12. I will get a point if the total is 5, 6, 7, 8, or 9." Roll the dice and keep a record of the score. The children should soon recognize that you are winning. Do not tell them why you are likely to be the winner even though you have only five sums to win on while they have six. Encourage them to find out why. (They should be ready for the experiment you just completed. Give interested children a record sheet and pair of dice. After they have completed their 50 rolls, discuss their findings. Let them figure out the probability for each sum to see why you were winning the competition.)

ACTIVITY 3

PICK-UP STICKS

The game of pick-up sticks has been popular for many years. You will use a can of pick-up sticks for a probability experiment. Unlike experiments in which coins or dice are used, so that you know the probability that a particular event will happen, this experiment uses a set of materials about which you know very little. You are to determine (as well as you can from the sampling you make) the content of the can and the probability of drawing a stick of each color.

| Colors | Samplings (50 draws per sar | | | | |
| | Sample 1 | | Sample 2 | | Sa |
	Tally	Total	Tally	Total	Ta
Red	II				
Yellow	I				

Make your own independent investigation. Do not work with a partner.

1. Ask your instructor for a set of pick-up sticks. Do not open the sealed container.

2. Remove the pick-up sticks record sheet from your manual (page 199).

3. Shake the container, then turn it so that a stick will fall through the hole in the lid.

4. Record the color of the stick on the top line of the left column of the record sheet. Also, put a tally mark on the same line in the column for Sample 1.

5. Return the stick to the container by putting it through the hole.

6. Repeat the process. If you get a stick colored the same as the first, put a second tally beside the first. If the stick is another color, write the color's name on the second line of the first column and put a tally mark following it in the Sample 1 column. Return the stick to the container.

7. Do this a total of 50 times.

8. Record the number of sticks of each color in the Total column.

9. Repeat the activity two more times, recording the data for each draw in the appropriate columns.

10. Complete the form by filling the blanks at the bottom.

11. Sign the form and give it to your instructor or the class member who is serving as collector.

DICE RECORD SHEET

SECOND DIE

	1	2	3	4	5	6
1						
2						
3						
4						
5						
6						

FIRST DIE

Each sum came up this many times:

2 _____   5 _____   8 _____   11 _____

3 _____   6 _____   9 _____   12 _____

4 _____   7 _____   10 _____

There are 36 different combinations. What is the probability of getting each sum?

2 _____   5 _____   8 _____   11 _____

3 _____   6 _____   9 _____   12 _____

4 _____   7 _____   10 _____

Signed _____

PICK-UP STICKS RECORD SHEET

There are 31 sticks in the container

Colors	Sample 1		Sample 2		Sample 3		Grand
	Tally	Total	Tally	Total	Tally	Total	Total

Samplings (50 draws per sample)

1. I believe there are more _____ sticks than of any other color.

2. I believe there are as many _____ sticks as there are _____ sticks.

3. I believe the _____ sticks are fewest in number.

4. My guesses for the number of sticks and odds for drawing one of each color are:

Color	Number	Odds
_____	_____	_____
_____	_____	_____
_____	_____	_____
_____	_____	_____
_____	_____	_____
_____	_____	_____

Signed _____

Total number of samplings _____
Total number of draws _____ (150 × number of samplings)
        Color   Number of each color drawn

        _____   _____
        _____   _____
        _____   _____
        _____   _____
        _____   _____
        _____   _____

After the pick-up sticks sheets for all class members have been collected, a complete record of the results will be made and given to you so that you can put the data on this form.

When you have data for all drawings, answer these questions:

1. What percentage of the total number of draws was the number of draws for each of the colors?

2. There are 31 sticks in the container; how many do you now guess there are of each color?

Color	%	Number in Container
____	____	_____
____	____	_____
____	____	_____
____	____	_____
____	____	_____
____	____	_____

3. List the odds for drawing a stick of each color.

ACTIVITY 4

SECRET CODE

The following coded message was sent by some children to another class across the hall:

ZU KTAU HUUF WUTPFBFC THXLV JPXHTHBWBVG
TFQ DVTVBDVBED. ZPBVBFC TFQ QUEBJKUPBFC
EXQUQ NUDDTCUD TPU ZTGD ZU KTAU WUTPFUQ
THXLV LDBFC JPXHTHBWBVG TFQ DVTVBDVBED.

With the coded message they sent the information contained in the chart on the next page. This information was obtained from an analysis they made of two groups of 73 words, beginning with the first word at the top of each of two pages selected at random from a textbook. It shows the frequency and percentage of use of each letter of the alphabet and the total number of letters in each 73-word passage. It also gives the total frequency of letters in both passages and the percentage of the total each is. (The process of rounding to the nearest tenth when figuring percentages accounts for the fact that none of the sums of percentages equals 100.) The children suggested that members of the other class might decode the message, using data from the word analysis as an aid to deciphering it. You are invited to do this, too. Decode the message and write it on the following lines.

_____

_____

_____

_____

_____

_____

_____

_____

_____

_____

The set of letter squares contains 24 pieces. Each piece differs from the others in one or more ways. Look at the large, plain *E* and the small plain *e*. They differ in *size*. Look at the large, plain *E* and the large, black *E*. They differ in *color*. Finally, look at the large, white *E* and the large, white *A*. They differ in *kind*. The set of letter squares has three distinguishing attributes—size, color, and kind.

You will use your letter squares for the next four activities.

ACTIVITY 5
ONE-DIFFERENCE CHAIN

This and the next activity focus on the letter squares' attributes, giving you opportunities to become thoroughly familiar with them.

1. Select one or two classmates with whom you will play.

2. Put a set of letter squares face down on the table; mix them well.

3. Each player draws an equal number of squares—12 if two are playing; 8 if three are playing. Do not show your pieces to your opponents.

4. The player chosen to initiate play puts a square face up on the table.

5. The player to his left selects one of his squares, one which differs from the first in one attribute only, and places it face up to the right of the first square.

6. Play continues as players take

FREQUENCY OF LETTERS FOUND IN ANALYSIS OF
TWO 73-WORD PASSAGES

Letter	First 73-word Passage		Second 73-word Passage		Combination of Two Passages	
	Number	Percent	Number	Percent	Total	Percent
A	21	6.2	34	8.4	55	7.4
B	5	1.5	6	1.5	11	1.5
C	11	3.2	20	4.9	31	4.2
D	16	4.7	23	5.7	39	5.2
E	59	17.3	55	13.6	114	15.3
F	6	1.8	5	1.2	11	1.5
G	1	0.3	6	1.5	7	0.9
H	18	5.3	20	4.9	38	5.1
I	18	5.3	33	8.1	51	6.8
J	0	0.0	0	0.0	0	0.0
K	0	0.0	2	0.5	2	0.3
L	14	4.1	19	4.7	33	4.4
M	8	2.3	7	1.7	15	2.0
N	24	7.0	37	9.1	61	8.3
O	27	7.9	23	5.7	50	6.7
P	9	2.6	3	0.7	12	1.6
Q	0	0.0	0	0.0	0	0.0
R	22	6.5	18	4.4	40	5.4
S	25	7.3	33	8.1	58	7.8
T	39	11.4	39	9.6	78	10.5
U	9	2.6	8	2.0	17	2.3
V	0	0.0	2	0.5	2	0.3
W	3	0.9	4	1.0	7	0.9
X	3	0.9	2	0.5	5	0.7
Y	4	1.2	5	1.2	9	1.2
Z	0	0.0	1	0.2	1	0.1
	341	100.3	405	99.6	746	100.4

turns putting their pieces down, making a chain of letters.

7. A player is blocked when he has no squares differing in only one attribute from the last-played piece. He loses his turn until he has a square that he can play.

8. The winner is the player who gets rid of all his pieces first.

Will any strategies help you win? Is it easier to win while playing a single opponent or two opponents?

Change the rules to make it a two-difference chain; a three-difference chain. Is any of the games easier to play than the others? Another variation is to place the squares in the form of a circle. The winner is the player who can close the circle by playing a square having one (or two, or three) difference(s) from both the last- and first-played squares.

Remove the square grid from your manual (page 205) and use it as the playing board for these games, which can be played as solitaire or with an opponent. Games on the grid require each player's attention to both one- and two-difference plays, as action moves both across and up and down the board.

1. Whether you are playing alone or against an opponent, play begins in the same way. Put a letter square in one of the squares of the grid. (The large, white A was played first in the example at right.)

2. The next play may be in either the square to the right or the left of the first, using a letter square differing in one way only from the first (as the small, white a in the example), or, above or below, using a letter square differing in two ways (as the large, black E).

3. Each successive play requires that a letter square differ in one way in the horizontal direction and in two ways in the vertical direction from each of those already played. In the example, a small, black e can be played in the square marked X. Are there any other letter squares that can be played in the same square?

ACTIVITY 6
SQUARE GRID GAMES

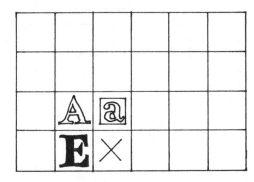

If you are playing solitaire, you play to rid yourself of all the letter squares. If you are playing an opponent, you play to rid yourself of squares before your opponent gets rid of his. (If play reaches a point at which neither player can put a piece on the board, the one having fewer letter squares is the winner.)

Make up some rules of your own for playing this game. What effect, if any, do your rules have on the difficulty of the game? For example, is it more difficult to win a game of solitaire?

You will need your letter squares, label cards, and string loops for these games, which focus attention on sorting and classifying the squares.

1. Arrange two loops to form overlapping rings.

2. Put one label card inside each of the rings.

3. Put letter squares inside or outside the rings, using the labels as guides to their placement.

4. When the game is played competitively, a point is awarded a player each time he places a letter square in its proper place. One player may challenge another when

ACTIVITY 7
VENN DIAGRAM GAMES

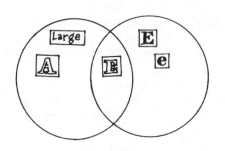

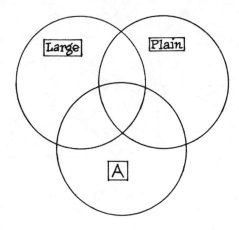

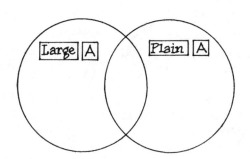

he believes a square has not been placed correctly. If he makes a proper challenge, he earns the point. Otherwise, the challenged player gets it, along with one of the challenger's points.

5. Repeat the game several times, using different label cards inside the loops for each game.

6. Use three loops and three label cards. Use two or three loops along with combinations of cards inside them.

Before you remove the label cards and letter squares at the end of each game, study the Venn diagram. Discussing the reasons for each piece's placement will help clarify a diagram's meaning. It is particularly helpful to consider questions like these:

1. What subset(s) of letter squares is (are) in the intersection(s) formed by the loops?

2. What subset(s) do you get when you form the union(s) of the subsets within the loops?

3. Are any empty sets found within the loops with this arrangement of labels and loops?

4. What subset of letter squares is outside all the loops? (Remember, the answer to this question cannot be none. Why?)

ACTIVITY 8
TREE NETWORKS

Tree networks (also called road networks) provide another means of sorting and classifying letter squares and other attribute materials. Your tree is a network of paper strips held together with brass fasteners. The simplest tree is one that is used to sort and classify elements contained in a set where there is but one distinguishing attribute and only two values, as in a set of checker pieces. The red pieces are put at the end of one branch; the black pieces are put at the end of the other one.

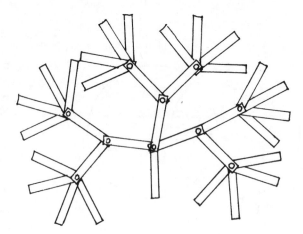

1. The tree at the right is one that can be used to sort and classify the letter squares.

2. Work with two classmates to make this tree. First remove the pages of strips from your manual. Cut along the lines to separate the strips, then punch one or two holes in each strip. Use paper fasteners to join the branches. Assemble the pictured tree.

3. Arrange one set of letter squares on the tree. Begin by putting all the squares at the base of the tree. Look up the trunk to where there are three branches. This tells you that you will separate the set by color— one color will go to each branch. Next see that each branch is separated so that there are two smaller branches. What attribute will you use at this point? Finally, each of the smaller branches separates into four more branches. What attribute is considered now? Your finished tree should have the large black letters at the ends of one set of four branches, the small black letters at the end of another set of four branches, and so on. Does it?

4. There are other ways the tree for letter squares can be formed. Use the other two sets of strips and letter squares to figure out how two of these trees will look, then sort your squares on the branches of each of the trees.

Tree networks can be used to introduce children to the idea of "either . . . or . . . ."

1. Form a tree as at right.

2. Make up a rule to guide your partner's placement of letter squares. For example, "Each letter square on the left-hand branch will be either an E or gray. All other squares will be on the right-hand branch."

3. Check your partner's arrangements of squares to see if they agree with the rule. Did he have any difficulty deciding where to place any of the squares? If so, which piece(s)? Why?

ACTIVITY 9

BOOKS AND COMMERCIAL MATERIALS

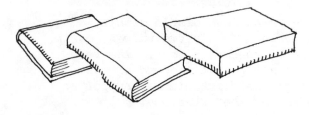

The first eight activities have introduced you to some of the experiences dealing with probability, statistics, and logic that children can have. Now you will become acquainted with books and commercially prepared materials dealing with these topics. The following list includes book titles and names of material kits.

1. Read some of the books.
2. Play some of the games and complete some of the investigations from commercially prepared kits.

STRIPS FOR TREES

STRIPS FOR TREES

STRIPS FOR TREES

BOOKS

Probability for Intermediate Grades: Teacher's Commentary. Rev. ed., 1966.

Presents a series of twelve lessons suitable for the nine- to twelve-year-old. The "Mathematical Comment" section gives the teacher background information, and the appendix describes probability devices.

Probability for Primary Grades: Teacher's Commentary. Rev. ed., 1966.

Presents a series of eleven lessons suitable for the six- to nine-year-old. Also has "Mathematical Comment" section and appendix.

Both of these books are by the School Mathematics Study Group and are available from:

> A. C. Vroman, Inc.
> 2085 E. Foothill Blvd.
> Pasadena, Ca. 91109

Statistics. 1967. By David S. Fielker.

This booklet, intended for children ten years old and up, shows how statistical information is organized and reported. It offers many suggestions for activities dealing with the subject.

> Cambridge University Press
> 32 East 57th Street
> New York, N.Y. 10022

Learning Logic, Logical Games. 1966. By Z. P. Dienes and E. W. Golding.

A set of forty-eight colored blocks are the playing pieces for the games, which are suited to children five to ten years old.

> Herder and Herder
> 232 Madison Avenue
> New York, N.Y. 10016

Sets, Probability, and Statistics. 1969. By Paul C. Clifford, Mildred Keiffer, and Max A. Sobel.

This free booklet describes probability investigations suitable for children ten years old and up. Applications of probability and statistics in the field of insurance are demonstrated.

> Educational Division
> Institute of Life Insurance
> 277 Park Avenue
> New York, N.Y. 10017

Checking Up 1. 1970.

The sections "Sets," "Inclusion," "Unions and Further Ideas on Inclusion," and "Intersection and Tables" offer useful suggestions for activities for the five- to eight-year-old.

Logic. No date.

The activities are intended for children six to twelve years old.

Mathematics: The First Three Years. 1970.

The number experiences described lay foundations for future work in all areas of mathematics. Activities dealing with sets and graphs are particularly helpful for developing understanding of logic and statistics.

Probability and Statistics. 1969.

Activities for children six to twelve years old are described.

These books are prepared in England by the Nuffield Foundation, where they are published by W & R Chambers and John Murray. (At the time this manual was published, *Logic* was in first-draft form and was not yet available for general distribution.) The U.S. distributor of Nuffield publications is:

> John Wiley & Sons, Inc.
> 605 Third Avenue
> New York, N.Y. 10016

Probability: A Programmed Supplement. 1969. By Donald D. Paige and Ian D. Beattie.

This booklet provides a 188-frame self-study program for elementary teachers who need background information about probability.

> Prindle, Weber & Schmidt, Inc.
> 53 State Street
> Boston, Mass. 02109

Probability and Statistics: An Introduction through Experiments. 1970. By Edmund C. Berkeley.

Investigations suitable for children ten years old and up are described.

> Berkeley Enterprises
> 815 Washington Street
> Newtonville, Mass. 02160

ATTRIBUTE MATERIALS

Math Matrix Games and Matrix Games for the five- to eight-year-old.

Appleton-Century-Crofts/New Century
Educational Division—Meredith Corp.
440 Park Avenue South
New York, N.Y. 10016

Dienes Logical Blocks (forty-eight pieces with sets available in three sizes)
and manual.

Herder and Herder
232 Madison Avenue
New York, N.Y. 10016

Attribute kits, ranging in size from sixty to ninety-six blocks, guides,
and other items; plastic tree and machine grids for sorting and classifying.

Math Media, Inc.
P.O. Box 345
Danbury, Conn. 06810

Attribute kit (sixty-block set), hoops, and teacher's guide.

Selective Educational Equipment, Inc.
Three Bridge Street
Newton, Mass. 02195

Attribute kit (sixty-block set), hoops and guide.

Teaching Resources
100 Boylston Street
Boston, Mass. 02116

Attribute kit (A Blocks, Color Cubes, People Pieces) and manual.

Webster Division
McGraw-Hill Book Company
Manchester Road
Manchester, Mo. 63011

PROBABILITY MATERIALS

"Forecast: An Introduction to the Science of Probability and Statistics."
A kit containing materials—dice, coin tossing machine, Hexstat device,
record sheets, etc.—and manual for probability and statistics experiments.

Math-Master
Box 1911
Big Springs, Texas 79720

ACTIVITY 10
CLASS DISCUSSION

The final activity is a class discussion about activities dealing with probability, statistics, and logic. Because these topics are new to elementary mathematics, their place in the program is not always understood or appreciated. If you have any questions about why you should concern children with activities like those in this chapter, now is the time to discuss them. Mosteller gives one reason for including study of probability and statistics in the curriculum. Use it as a basis for initiating the discussion.

Some may feel that this sort of material [investigations into probability and statistics] is only for the youth who is quick at science and mathematics, and certainly such a youngster will profit mightily. But it is not so well known that children retarded in the mathematical areas brighten up when presented mathematical tasks derived from experiments that they have executed themselves—an interest they do not show for similar sets of data gathered by others. The concreteness of the numbers and the personal motivation to make something of their own unique experiment gives a lift to the arithmetic and to their understanding. And if you work with such a youngster, see if you can spend most of your time in praise and in noticing what is right, a little in finding new ways for *him* to find his own mistakes, and *none* in showing how quickly you can do the same work.[1]

---

[1] Reprinted with permission from the foreword by Frederick Mosteller to Edmund C. Berkeley's *Probability and Statistics: An Introduction through Experiments* ([815 Washington St.], Newtonville, Mass. [02160]: Berkeley Enterprises, 1970). (Emphasis in original.)

APPENDIX A

Elementary School Mathematics. Rev. ed., 1971. By Eicholz, O'Daffer, and Martin.

K-6; teacher's and pupils' editions, readiness and test booklets for grades three through six, workbooks for grades three through six, duplicating masters for grades one through six, manipulative aids, Spanish edition for entire series.

Mathematics for Schools. 1970 (Level I); 1971 (Level II). By Fletcher.

Level I consists of seven consumable books for five- to seven-year-olds and a teacher's resource book; Level II has nonconsumable books for eight- to eleven-year-olds. Activity-oriented program developed in England and based on the Nuffield mathematics project.

> Addison-Wesley Publishing Company
> Sand Hill Road
> Menlo Park, Ca. 94025

Mathematics in Action. 1969. By Deans, Kane, McMeen, Oesterle, Beigel, Evans, Fejfar, Goodfellow, and Jackson.

1-8; teacher's and pupils' editions, activity and duplicating masters for grades three through eight, achievement/placement tests for grades one through eight.

> American Book Company
> 300 Pike Street
> Cincinnati, Ohio 45202

Heath Elementary Mathematics. 1972. By Dilley, Rucker, and Jackson.

K-6; teacher's and pupils' editions, duplicating masters for basic and supplementary worksheets for grades one through six, drill and practice cassettes and tests for grades three through six.

New Ways in Numbers. 2d ed., 1969. By Hatzo, Horrigan, and Smith.

1-8; teacher's and pupils' editions, paperbound workbook series.

> D. C. Heath and Company
> Raytheon Education Corporation
> 2700 North Richardt Avenue
> Indianapolis, Ind. 46219

Ginn Elementary Mathematics. 1972. By Scott, Immerzeel, Wiederanders, MacPherson, Moulton, and Ames.

   1-8; teacher's and pupils' editions, duplicating masters for levels one through eight, activity books for levels three through six, tests for all levels.

> Ginn and Company
> P.O. Box 191
> Boston, Mass. 02107

Mathematics. 2d ed., 1968. By Payne, Wells, Spooner, Clark, Beatty, and May.

   K-6; teacher's and pupils' editions.

Harbrace Mathematics. 1972. By Payne, May, Beatty, Wells, Spooner, and Cominy.

   K-6; teacher's and pupils' editions, workbooks, duplicating masters, and study prints.

> Harcourt Brace Jovanovich, Inc.
> 757 Third Avenue
> New York, N.Y. 10017

New Dimensions in Mathematics. 1970. By D'Augustine, Brown, Heddens, and Howard.

   K-6; teacher's and pupils' editions, readiness books and laboratory materials for preschool and kindergarten, duplicating masters for grades one through six, workbooks for grades three through six.

> Harper & Row, Publishers
> 2500 Crawford Avenue
> Evanston, Ill. 60201

Elementary Mathematics: Patterns and Structure. 1968. By Flournoy, Nichols, Kalin, and Simon.

   1-8; teacher's and pupils' editions, duplicating masters for grades one and two, Spanish language exercise books for grades one and two, workbooks for grades three through eight, tests for grades three through eight, filmstrips for grades three through seven, three-book accelerated sequence for selected pupils after completion of grade four text.

Exploring Elementary Mathematics. 1970. By Keedy, Dwight, Nelson, Schluep, and Anderson.

   K-6; teacher's and pupils' editions, workbooks and test booklets for grades three through six, duplicating masters for grades one and two.

Holt, Rinehart and Winston, Inc.
383 Madison Avenue
New York, N.Y. 10017

Modern School Mathematics. Rev. ed., 1972. By Duncan, Capps, Dolciani, Quast, and Zweng.

K-8; teacher's and pupils' editions, duplicating masters and overhead visuals for grades one through eight, diagnostic tests, workbooks, and manipulative aids for grades one through six, programmed practice for grades three through eight, progress tests for grades seven and eight, solution keys for grades five through eight.

Houghton Mifflin Company
110 Tremont Street
Boston, Mass. 02107

The Understanding Mathematics Program. 1971-72. By Nesbit, Pearson, Wallen, Gundlach, Buffie, Denny, and Kempf.

K-8; teacher's and pupils' editions, practice exercise books, tests, and related aids.

Laidlaw Brothers
Doubleday & Company, Inc.
Thatcher and Madison
River Forest, Ill. 60305

Developing Mathematics, K-8. 1970. By Phillips, Thoburn, Sanders, and Fitzgerald.

K-8; teacher's and pupils' editions, workbooks for grades three through eight.

The Macmillan Company
School Division
866 Third Avenue
New York, N.Y. 10022

Mastering Mathematics. 1970. By Davis, Farmer, Gladstone, Goode, Hadler, Halliday, Pollack, Scaffa, Schmidtmann, Sussman, Tobin, and Weiss.

K-8; workbook series.

The Random House Mathematics Program. 1972. By Suppes, Smith, Easterday, Firl, Carr, Kaplan, Phillips, and Brederhorn.

K-6; teacher's and pupils' editions, duplicating masters for kindergarten through grade two, workbooks for grades three through six.

Random House
School Division
201 East 50th Street
New York, N.Y. 10022

Sadlier Contemporary Mathematics. 1971. By Bezuszka, Halliday, Weiss, Newman, Goode, McDonnell, Grossman, and McDonnell.

K-9; teacher's and pupils' write-in books.

W. H. Sadlier, Inc.
11 Park Place
New York, N.Y. 10007

Greater Cleveland Mathematics Program. Rev. ed., 1968. By the Educational Research Council of America.

K-6; teacher's and pupils' editions, write-in texts in addition to hardcover for grades three through six, manipulative aids for kindergarten through grade three.

Science Research Associates
259 East Erie Street
Chicago, Ill. 60611

Seeing through Arithmetic. 1969. By Hartung, Van Engen, Gibb, Stochl, Knowles, Walch, and Castaneda.

K-6; teacher's and pupils' editions, test and practice booklets for grades one through six, duplicating masters for grades three through six.

Scott, Foresman and Company
1900 East Lake Avenue
Glenview, Ill. 60025

Modern Mathematics through Discovery. Rev. ed., 1970. By Morton, Gray, Rosskopf, Moredock, Collins, Sage, Trafton, and Sinard.

K-8; teacher's and pupils' editions, skills practice books and achievement tests for grades three through seven, manipulative aids for kindergarten through grade three.

Silver Burdett Company
General Learning Corporation
Box 362
Morristown, N.J. 07960

Elementary Mathematics: Concepts, Properties, and Operations. 1970. By
    Spitzer, Banks, Burns, Kahrs, and Folsom.

    K-8; teacher's and pupils' editions, duplicating masters for grades
one and two, workbooks for grades three through eight.

                Webster Division
                McGraw-Hill Book Company
                Manchester Road
                Manchester, Mo. 63011

APPENDIX B

MATHEMATICS LABORATORY MATERIALS

Materials for equipping a mathematics laboratory are available in many kinds and from many companies. Some are listed here under the following headings: Activity Cards, Film Loops, Films, Filmstrips and Slide Programs, Games and Puzzles, Mathematics Kits, Records, Tape Programs, and Transparencies. The materials are representative of those currently available; it is not possible to include everything on the market. Companies are listed in alphabetical order under each heading.

Activity Cards

"Developmental Math Cards."

Twelve sets, two for each grade, one through six, with twenty to twenty-two cards containing ideas for open-ended investigations.

> Addison-Wesley Publishing Company
> Sand Hill Road
> Menlo Park, Ca. 94025

"Student Activity Cards for Cuisenaire Rods."

Sixty-three activity cards for exploring arithmetic with Cuisenaire rods.

> Cuisenaire Company of America, Inc.
> 12 Church Street
> New Rochelle, N.Y. 10805

"Problems: Green Set"; "Problems: Purple Set"; "Problems: Red Set."

Each set contains problem cards and a teacher's guide; wide range of topics; from Britain's Nuffield mathematics project.

> John Wiley & Sons, Inc.
> 605 Third Avenue
> New York, N.Y. 10016

"LRA Math Mates" (activity cards).

Presents activities dealing with a variety of devices, including abacus, balance, number boards, attribute blocks; devices also available.

> Learning Research Associates, Inc.
> 1501 Broadway
> New York, N.Y. 10036

"Macmillan Math Activity Cards."

Grouped into five instructional levels for grades two through six; deal with five basic topics: graphs, shapes, measurements, patterns, and games.

The Macmillan Company
School Division
866 Third Avenue
New York, N.Y. 10022

Film Loops

Four- or five-film sets covering addition, subtraction, multiplication, and division.

American Film Productions, Inc.
1540 Broadway
New York, N.Y. 10036

More than forty titles covering a range of topics for all grades.

Association-Sterling Films
600 Madison Avenue
New York, N.Y. 10022

Dienes Arithmetic Films.

Nineteen super 8mm color films dealing with structure of numeration and elementary operations, based on Dienes's approach to mathematics learning.

Herder and Herder
232 Madison Avenue
New York, N.Y. 10016

Elementary Geometry: Forms We See

Five films with study guides.

Hester and Associates
11422 Harry Hines, #212
Dallas, Texas 75229

Twenty-four titles covering a range of topics for all grades.

Jott Films
P.O. Box 745
Belmont, Ca. 94002

Macmillan Elementary Math Film Loops

Forty super 8mm color films covering topics commonly taught in elementary school.

The Macmillan Company
School Division
866 Third Avenue
New York, N.Y. 10022

Twenty-four titles covering a range of topics for all grades.

> Sterling Educational Films
> 241 East 34th Street
> New York, N.Y. 10016

Films

Let's Measure series.

Four films dealing with linear, weight, and liquid measure and standard units for primary grades.

> Coronet Instructional Films
> 65 E. South Water Street
> Chicago, Ill. 60601

Dance Squared; How Do You Count?; The Idea of Number; Notes on a Triangle; and *Trio for Three Angles*.

> International Film Bureau, Inc.
> 332 S. Michigan Avenue
> Chicago, Ill. 60604

Elementary Mathematics for Teachers and Students.

Twelve teacher and thirty-nine student films covering a variety of topics, produced by the National Council of Teachers of Mathematics.

> Silver Burdett Company
> General Learning Corporation
> Box 362
> Morristown, N.J. 07960

Modern Elementary Mathematics Series.

Six films: *Equations; Inverse Operations; Associativity; Commutativity; Inequalities;* and *Sets and Numbers*.

> Webster Division
> McGraw-Hill Book Company
> Manchester Road
> Manchester, Mo. 63011

Filmstrips and Slide Programs

"Measuring Things."

Set of six color filmstrips with sound.

> Coronet Instructional Films
> 65 E. South Water Street
> Chicago, Ill. 60601

"Kenner on Modern Mathematics."

    Forty-eight color filmstrips grouped into twelve series for grades one through six.

"Learning New Numbers."

    Set of sixteen color filmstrips on common and decimal fractions.

"Learning to Measure."

    Set of four color filmstrips.

"Nature of Geometry."

    Set of four color filmstrips.

> Filmstrip House
> 432 Park Avenue
> New York, N.Y. 10016

"Harbrace Mathematics Instructional Slides."

    Seven hundred slides for daylight blackboard projection covering a range of topics for grades three through six.

> Harcourt Brace Jovanovich, Inc.
> 757 Third Avenue
> New York, N.Y. 10017

"Elementary Mathematics: Patterns and Structure."

    Forty-seven filmstrips grouped into five series.

> Holt, Rinehart and Winston, Inc.
> 383 Madison Avenue
> New York, N.Y. 10017

"Mathematics for Children."

    Set of four color filmstrips.

> Hudson Photographic Industries, Inc.
> 25 Buckhout Street
> Irvington-on-Hudson, N.Y. 10533

"Fun with Sets."

    Set of two color filmstrips with sound.

"Problems in Addition."

    One hundred seven frame color filmstrip (also have one each for subtraction, multiplication, and division).

                         International Film Bureau, Inc.
                         332 S. Michigan Avenue
                         Chicago, Ill. 60604

"Situational Math."

    Set of thirty color filmstrips with sound.

                         Knowledge Aid
                         Division of MJE Corporation
                         6633 West Howard Street
                         Niles, Ill. 60648

"Mathstrip."

    Three sets, each with forty-eight mathstrips: "The Number Facts";
"Per Cent: Rounding Off, Place Value"; and "Shortened Multiplying and
Dividing by 10, 100, 1000."

"Set Theory."

    One color filmstrip.

                         Library Filmstrip Center
                         3033 Aloma
                         Wichita, Kan. 67211

"Adventure with Numbers."

    Set of six color filmstrips.

"Arithmetic."

    Eighteen color filmstrips grouped into three series.

"Calendar Study."

    Set of six color filmstrips.

"History of Measures."

    Set of six black and white filmstrips.

"Measuring Length."

    Set of six color filmstrips.

"Modern Arithmetic."

    Thirty-six color filmstrips grouped into six series for kindergarten
through grade six.

"New Horizons in Arithmetic."

    Set of seven color filmstrips.

McGraw-Hill Films
330 West 42nd Street
New York, N.Y. 10036

"Discovering with the Number Line."

Set of ten color filmstrips.

"Mathematics for Primary Grades."

Set of eight color filmstrips.

"Numbers, Names and Colors."

Set of five color filmstrips with visual aids.

"Using Sets and Numbers."

Set of ten color filmstrips.

Scott Educational Division
104 Lower Westerfield Road
Holyoke, Mass. 01040

"Arithmetic Combinations."

Set of four black and white filmstrips.

"Understanding Fractions."

Set of eight color filmstrips.

"Using Modern Mathematics."

Forty-nine color filmstrips grouped into six series for grades one through six.

Society for Visual Education
1345 Diversey Parkway
Chicago, Ill. 60614

Games and Puzzles

Math Games and Puzzles Kit #1.

Contains geoboard, pyramid, strip, triangle, and tangram puzzles; activity cards and teacher's guide also available.

Concept Company, Inc.
P.O. Box 273
Belmont, Mass. 02178

"Tuf"; "Kalah"; "Krypto"; "Numble"; "Equations"; and "Tri-Nim."

These and other games encourage children to think about strategies for winning, help them understand logic, and give them practice in making equations.

> Creative Publications
> P.O. Box 328
> Palo Alto, Ca. 94302

"Playing Card Number Games"; "Spinner Number Games"; and "Domino Number Games."

Each with guide, instruction cards, and storage box.

> D. C. Heath and Company
> 2700 North Richardt Avenue
> Indianapolis, Ind. 46219

"Deck-A-Dot."

Kit of eight card games for building mathematical readiness, plastic cardholder racks, and teacher's manual.

> EduGame Learning Aids, Inc.
> Dept. D
> 404 Scott Avenue
> Syracuse, N.Y. 13224

"Imout."

Games dealing with addition and subtraction, multiplication and division, and fractions.

> Imout Arithmetic Drill Games
> 706 Williamson Building
> Cleveland, Ohio 44114

"Mathaid" Games: "Arithmecubes," and "Orbiting the Earth," and "Geoshapes," "I Win," and "Polyhedron Rummy" card games.

> Scott, Foresman and Company
> 1900 East Lake Avenue
> Glenview, Ill. 60025

"Nine Man Morris"; "Back Up Three"; "Chinese Friends"; and other ancient games and puzzles.

> World Wide Games
> Box 450
> Delaware, Ohio 43015

Geoboards

Cuisenaire Geoboard.

Five by five array of pegs on one side with a seventeen-peg circle arrangement on the other, Geocards, recording sheets, transparent board, and *Notes on Geoboards* and *Geoboard Geometry* guidebooks.

> Cuisenaire Company of America, Inc.
> 12 Church Street
> New Rochelle, N.Y. 10805

Ideal Geoboard.

Geoboard is 7-1/2 inches square with five by five array of pegs; twenty-two lessons on duplicator masters.

> Gamco Industries, Inc.
> Box 1911 B
> Big Springs, Texas 79720

Houghton Mifflin Geoboard.

Seven inches square with six by six array of pegs on one side and two concentric circles on the other; forty-two student Geocards.

> Houghton Mifflin Company
> 110 Tremont Street
> Boston, Mass. 02107

Sigma Geosquare.

Geoboards, square and circular, ten inches square with five by five array on the square board, also in transparent plexiglas; teacher's guide.

> Sigma Division of Scott Scientific, Inc.
> Box 2121
> Fort Collins, Colo. 80521

Walker Geo-Board.

Five by five array of pegs, teacher's guide, and Geo-Cards.

> Walker
> 720 Fifth Avenue
> New York, N.Y. 10019

"Math Modules."

Seven skill boxes for grades one through seven, covering eight learning areas: numeration/place value; addition/subtraction; multiplication/division; fractions; decimals; geometry; special topics; and measurement. Includes all components needed for individualizing children's learning experiences.

> Appleton-Century-Crofts/New Century
> Educational Division—Meredith Corporation
> 440 Park Avenue
> New York, N.Y. 10016

"Arithmetic Step by Step."

Kit A provides activities for kindergarten through grade two; Kit B provides for grades three through six. Each kit contains ten units with three levels per unit, teacher's guide; duplicator master format.

> The Continental Press, Inc.
> Elizabethtown, Pa. 17022

"New Cuisenaire Classroom Kit."

Contains twenty-four student sets of Cuisenaire rods. Other kits and guidebooks, such as *Using the Cuisenaire Rods* and *Mathematics with Numbers in Color*, are also available.

> Cuisenaire Company of America, Inc.
> 12 Church Street
> New Rochelle, N.Y. 10805

"Continuous Progress Laboratory: Mathematics."

Eight kits, one for each grade one through eight; each contains approximately 350 cards, eight reel or cassette tapes, student progress books, test books, teacher resource units and guides, correlation chart, and pupil progress poster.

> Education Progress Corporation
> 8538 East 41st Street
> Tulsa, Okla. 74145

"Stern Structural Arithmetic Apparatus."

Materials for providing readiness and early number experiences, developed by Catherine Stern.

> Educational Teaching Aids Division
> A. Daigger and Company
> 159 W. Kinzie Street
> Chicago, Ill. 60610

"Polyhedron Model Kit."

Kit contains die-cut cardstock paper for models, instruction booklet, and *Polyhedron Models for the Classroom*, by Wenninger.

Gamco Industries, Inc.
Box 1911
Big Springs, Texas 79720

"Multibase Arithmetic Blocks."

Set contains materials for investigations of bases 3, 4, 5, and 6, work cards, and teacher's manual, developed by Z. P. Dienes.

Herder and Herder
232 Madison Avenue
New York, N.Y. 10016

"Early Childhood Curriculum."

Three kits: "Classification"; "Number Measurement and Space"; and "Seriation." Includes professional book and teacher's guide.

Learning Research Associates, Inc.
1501 Broadway
New York, N.Y. 10036

"Mathematics Involvement Program."

Kit contains activity cards and manipulatives to provide active learning experiences in kindergarten through grade six; teacher's handbook.

Science Research Associates
259 East Erie Street
Chicago, Ill. 60611

"Mathkit."

Contains materials for mathematics laboratory emphasizing active learning for children in kindergarten through grade three.

Silver Burdett Company
General Learning Corporation
Box 362
Morristown, N.J. 07960

"Individualizing Mathematics: Drill and Practice Kits."

Four kits containing cards grouped by topics; provides drill and practice covering topics commonly taught in elementary school.

Singer/Random House
School Division
201 East 50th Street
New York, N.Y. 10022

Records

"Bremner Multiplication Records."

Five records, with music, provide practice on multiplication with factors 2 through 12; 33-1/3 and 45 rpm.

> Bremner Multiplication Records
> Wilmette, Ill. 60091

"The New Math."

Eight albums emphasizing concepts and structure covering a range of topics; 33-1/3 rpm.

> RCA Educational Sales
> 1133 Avenue of the Americas
> New York, N.Y. 10036

"Math Skills Program."

Five records provide drill for addition, subtraction, multiplication, division, and a combination of these operations.

> Teaching Aids Institute
> 423 South Hindry Avenue
> Inglewood, Ca. 90301

Tape Programs

"The Abacus."

Set consists of cassette tape, abacus, and teacher guide card.

> Acoustifone Corporation
> Marketing Department
> 20149 Sunburst Street
> Chatsworth, Ca. 91311

"Merrill Mathematics Skilltapes."

Forty cassette tapes, nine student booklets, and teacher's guide.

> Charles E. Merrill Publishing Co.
> A Bell & Howell Company
> 1300 Alum Creek Drive
> Columbus, Ohio 43216

"Countdown."

Fifty lessons on cassette tapes with student response sheets, for grades one through three.

The Economy Company
P.O. Box 25308
Oklahoma City, Okla. 73125

"Explora Tapes: Math."

Sixty reel or cassette tapes presenting 120 enrichment lessons, for grades three through eight.

Educational Progress Corporation
8538 East 41st Street
Tulsa, Okla. 74145

"Minisystems Elementary Mathematics Series."

Structured, sequenced program with 100 cassettes or reels grouped into seven levels and covering basic concepts for kindergarten through grade six.

Electronic Futures, Inc.
57 Dodge Avenue
North Haven, Conn. 06473

"Primary Math Skills Improvement Program" and "Intermediate Math Program."

Two cassette programs, each containing forty tapes, student response booklets, teacher's manual, and placement test kit.

Imperial International Learning Corporation
Box 548
Kankakee, Ill. 60901

"Motivations in Mathematics."

Four recordings on reel or cassette tapes or records: "Math in the Future"; "The Idea of Ten"; "Musing Mathematicians"; and "Mousical Mathematics."

H. Wilson
555 West Taft Drive
South Holland, Ill. 60473

"Math Mastery Tapes."

Two programs: "Number and Numeration," fifteen tapes; and "Introduction to Fraction Concepts," eight tapes; work-study guides for each unit.

Learning Research Associates, Inc.
1501 Broadway
New York, N.Y. 10036

"Drilltapes."

Eighty reels or cassettes with two teacher's guides, for grades one through eight.

Science Research Associates
259 East Erie Street
Chicago, Ill. 60611

"Basic Number Concepts."

Contains four reel or cassette tapes, twenty transparencies, and fourteen spirit master worksheets.

"Modern Math Concepts."

Twenty-three tapes with student worksheets covering sets, equation solving, perimeter, area, and volume, and algebra.

Tapes Unlimited
13001 Puritan Avenue
Detroit, Mich. 48227

"Wollensak Teaching Tapes: Mathematics."

More than sixty reel or cassette tapes covering a range of topics for grades one through six.

Wollensak
Mincom Division of 3M Company
3M Center
St. Paul, Minn. 55101

Transparencies

"Math Master" Programs.

For grades one through six, with from sixty-three to as many as ninety-one transparencies per set, covering topics commonly taught in each grade. This company also has sets dealing with arithmetic skills, fractions, area, and other topics.

Gamco Industries, Inc.
P.O. Box 1911 A
Big Springs, Texas 79720

"Modern School Mathematics" Overhead Visuals.

Eight sets, each containing twenty-five to twenty-eight visuals plus overlays, geared to this company's mathematics textbook series for grades one through eight.

Houghton Mifflin Company
110 Tremont Street
Boston, Mass. 02107

"Basic Sets (One-by-One)."

Nine projectuals, plus mount with movable abacus.

"Down the Math Path: Basic Addition and Subtraction."

    Thirty-five transparencies, one record, and twenty-five spirit masters.

"Down the Math Path: Sets."

    Thirty-eight transparencies, one record, and thirty spirit masters.

"Number Facts Review."

    Vol. 1, Addition and Subtraction, thirty-eight transparencies.
    Vol. 2, Multiplication and Division, thirty-two transparencies.

            Scott Education Division
            104 Lower Westerfield Road
            Holyoke, Mass. 01040

"Chalkboard Transparencies."

    Thirty transparencies dealing with number line, grids, hundreds squares, circles, magic squares, and other patterns. The set is unique in that each transparency projects a white image on the chalkboard, so that the projected image can be marked.

            Scott Scientific, Inc.
            Box 2121
            Fort Collins, Colo. 80521

"Visualizing Elementary Mathematics."

    Two kits containing projectuals covering a variety of topics; teacher's manual.

            Singer/Random House
            School Division
            201 East 60th Street
            New York, N.Y. 10022

"Modern Mathematics."

    Seventy-eight transparencies grouped into seven series for primary grades.

            United Transparencies Incorporated
            P.O. Box 688
            Binghamton, N.Y. 13902

"Modern Math Series II."

    Forty transparencies, with carrying case and teacher's manual, covering operations, place value, long division, geometry, measurement, and clock arithmetic.

            Visual Materials, Inc.
            Redwood City, Ca. 94063

INDIVIDUAL CHECKSHEET

This checksheet contains a list of different things you are to be able to do before you complete this book. As you learn a skill or complete a task, have a classmate check you and then initial the right-hand column. You are not to ask a classmate to initial your checksheet until you have demonstrated to him how to use the device or play the game. A minimum of two items must be demonstrated for and initialed by the instructor. You may choose which two, then let him know when you are ready to demonstrate your understanding of the device, skill, and so on.

Device and/or Game	How I Demonstrated My Understanding of It	Initials
1. I can represent any 3-place number on an abacus and with beansticks (p. 38, "Whole Numbers").		
2. I can use the abacus and beansticks to illustrate addition, with and without regrouping (pp. 49-50, "Whole Numbers").		
3. I can use the abacus and beansticks to illustrate subtraction, with and without regrouping (pp.50-52, "Whole Numbers").		
4. I can use markers to illustrate the repeated addition and array interpretations of multiplication (pp. 55, 61, "Whole Numbers").		

Device and/or Game	How I Demonstrated My Understanding of It	Initials
5. I have played some variations of the chain and square grid games (pp.202, 204-205, "Probability, Statistics, and Logic").		
6. I can make the two "tree" networks for the letter squares (pp. 207-208, "Probability, Statistics, and Logic").	Describe each of your trees.	
7. I have played some of the games described in these books_____ _____ _____ _____ (pp. 215-216, "Probability, Statistics, and Logic").	These are the games:	